The
Write
Stuff

Learn How To Write Better
Right Now With The Approach
That Combines Creativity
And Computer Logic

By Harley Bjelland

THE CAREER PRESS
180 FIFTH AVE.
PO BOX 34
HAWTHORNE, NJ 07507
1-800-CAREER-1
201-427-0229 (OUTSIDE U.S.)
FAX: 201-427-2037

THE WRITE STUFF Learn How to Write Better *Right Now* With the Approach That Combines Creativity and Computer Logic

ISBN 0-934829-86-1, $9.95

Cover design by The Electronic Studio

Copies of this volume may be ordered by mail or phone directly from the publisher. To order by mail, please include price as noted above, $2.50 handling per order, as well as $1.00 for each book ordered. Send to: The Career Press, Inc., 180 Fifth Ave., P.O. Box 34, Hawthorne, N.J. 07507

Or call Toll-free 1-800-CAREER-1 (in Canada: 201-427-0229) to order using your VISA or MasterCard or for further information on all books published or distributed by The Career Press.

To the continuing joys of my life,
my beloved grandchildren:

Kristen Sueoka
Jennifer Bjelland
Elizabeth Bjelland
Christina Welch
Matthew Sueoka
Sara Bjelland
Tara Bjelland
Hayley Sueoka
Harley Bjelland II
...and more to come, I hope.

Contents

The
Write
Stuff

Introduction
Writing That Blooms   11

Chapter 1
Order: The Basis For Modular Writing   15

Chapter 2
Organize and the Writing is Easy   35

Chapter 3
The P-Sort: A New Way to Organize   49

Chapter 4
Order Out of Chaos: Two Examples   57

Chapter 5
Brainstorming: Exercising Your Creativity   71

Chapter 6
The PC: A Writer's Most Valuable Tool   91

Chapter 7
Research: How to Find Information Fast   97

Chapter 8
The Magic Three Elements of Writing   117

Chapter 9
The Universal Top-down Design Subroutine   131

Chapter 10
Top-down Design For a Short Story/Article   145

Chapter 11
Bottom-up Writing Subroutine for the Short   155

Chapter 12
Bottom-up Writing: Two Examples   169

Chapter 13
Good Writing Techniques   181

Afterword
A Little Feedback, Please   197

Appendix A
References and Sources   199

Appendix B
Addresses of On-line Vendors   215

Appendix C
Bibliography   217

Index
The Write Stuff   219

Acknowledgements

Thank You

Thanks to my wife, Dorrie, for her continued patience and tolerance of my prolonged isolation periods. It's always a long and somewhat lonely journey from the kernel of an idea to a completed book and I'm grateful for the companionship along the way.

Many thanks to Ron Fry, president of Career Press, for his belief in the book, his encouragement, and the intriguing title of the book. And special kudos to Betsy Sheldon, editor in chief of Career Press, for serving as an excellent and questioning test-base for the book. She made many excellent suggestions for improvement.

This book was written using Microsoft Word on Freya, my classical new Macintosh Classic. Many thanks to Ron Setterholm, instructor par-excellence, of Lane Community College, who showed me how to speak the "language" and "mouse" my way around the Mac. Thanks, Freya, for taking so much of the drudgery out of writing.

I also owe a deep debt of gratitude to the many unnamed creative computer pioneers who devised programming techniques that show how to accomplish things in a logical and orderly manner and help to create order out of chaos. Some of the techniques in this book resulted from these computer programming principles.

"If a man empties his purse into his head, no one can take it away from him. An investment in knowledge always pays the best investment."

Benjamin Franklin

Writing
That
Blooms

Full many a gem of purest ray serene,
The dark unfathom'd caves of ocean bear;
Full many a flower is born to blush unseen
And waste its sweetness on the desert air.
Anon.

This book is targeted at helping you create writing that shines and blooms, delivering its sweetness for all to savor. The techniques described apply to both fiction and nonfiction manuscripts ranging in length from letters to full-length books.

Many of the ideas and concepts in this book are unique with the author. Two of these unique concepts are:

- The Precedent Sort and
- Modular Writing.

The Precedent Sort, or P-Sort, is a logical, easy-to-use method of organizing material *prior* to writing. Modular Writing is a procedure that complements the Precedent Sort. These two unique concepts permit writing your masterpieces in an order that is optimum for you, and help you maintain the continuity and logical organization that are so essential to good writing. Modular Writing helps defeat "writer's block" that, from time to time, plagues most writers.

Although we have many modern computer programs at our disposal, these aides have only succeeded in computerizing some of the more onerous writing tasks. Modern technology is of no use unless people can write and communicate clearly, effectively, and accurately. And not even the most sophisticated computer program can transform poor writing into good.

One area of writing that has not been enhanced by computers are the initial and very important steps of creating and outlining the raw material for a short story, an article, or a book and developing a systematic plan for designing (outlining) the manuscript and writing the text. The Precedent Sort and Modular Writing, along with Top-down Design and Bottom-up Writing Subroutines described in this book, provide new techniques for accomplishing these vital parts of the writing process.

How to read this book

The Write Stuff was designed to be read from beginning-to-end. The chapters form a series of logical, sequential activities that show you, step-by-step, how to research, organize, and write both fiction and nonfiction manuscripts of any length.

To use this book most effectively, first scan the Table of Contents to get a quick outline of the entire book, the subjects covered, and the extent to which they're discussed. A large number of visuals are included throughout the book to enhance your understanding of the techniques and principles covered. Look over the illustrations to see another aspect of the book's content.

Then begin with Chapter 1 and read the entire chapter. This initial chapter gives you a good introduction to the many topics, plus an outline of each chapter's contents. The Precedent Sort and Modular Writing are introduced in this chapter. These unique concepts promise to make writing easier for you and will help you create more readable, more informative, more saleable manuscripts. Adapted from computer programming principles, The Precedent Sort and Modular Writing simplify and put order into the basic writing processes.

The subsequent chapters describe the Precedent Sort in detail and show how it can be used for both fiction and nonfiction. An entire chapter is then devoted to the creative and essential part of writing, brainstorming. Later chapters describe how to research topics for your writing using not only the libraries, but also the online databases that are capturing and making available to you, via your personal computer, much of what is being printed today.

The "Magic Three," the Beginning, the Middle, and the End, are then covered and techniques are described that show how to incorporate these three basic parts into *every* type of writing you accomplish.

Top-down design and Bottom-up writing subroutines are introduced and examples are given of how to use these techniques to research, outline, design and write both fiction and nonfiction. The book concludes with a chapter on good writing techniques, a quick overview on what it takes to accomplish good writing.

Be an active reader

When you read this book, be an active reader. Keep a marking pen nearby and underline or highlight the points you would particularly like to upload into your personal memory bank. This also helps you relocate the important points that you may want to return to and review later.

Complete the exercises at the ends of each chapter. These exercises were designed to reinforce and expand on what you have read by practicing the principles taught.

This book was written not just to be *read*, this book was written to be *used*. So, use it well and you'll find that your fiction and nonfiction writing will be easier to create, a delight to write, entertaining, and informative.

May you have much pleasant and profitable reading and may you learn how to make your writing shine for the whole world to see.

Chapter 1

Order: The Basis for Modular Writing

"Order and simplification are the first steps toward the mastery of a subject."
Thomas Mann

Writers are made, not born. That's what this book is all about: making writers.

If your mind bursts with exciting ideas and you want to learn how to capture and organize them into some logical form, this book is for you. If you want to learn how to brainstorm, research, collect your thoughts and write them up into a readable article, a short story, a report, a novel, or a nonfiction book, this text will help you accomplish that goal. If you've read bad writing that gets published and know you can write better, this step-by-step manual will help you prove your claim. If you've had a wide variety of good and bad experiences, possess strong beliefs, and experience fantastic imaginings, this book will help you cull, organize, and write them up into a publishable form so you can tell (and *sell*) your story to the world.

Because this book is about taking your ideas, your memories, your knowledge, your inspirations, your disasters, your triumphs, your thoughts, your loves, your hopes, and your hates and converting this valuable and unique raw material into prose. You are the sole person in the entire world who possesses this raw material. You have a unique lifetime of living and learning and reading stored in your memory. You are the only individual who can shape this one-of-a-kind product into the logical form needed for it to be published. This book will show you how to retrieve, massage, and mold this valuable material and will help guide you through the misty maze that lies between your brainstorms and the printed page.

Computers revolutionize writing

"Next to doing things that deserve to be written, nothing gets a man more credit, or gives him more pleasure than to write things that deserve to be read."
Earl of Chesterfield

Personal computers are revolutionizing many aspects of the writing process. Modern word-processing programs format, display, store for easy recall and effortless editing, and flawlessly print out your manuscripts. Complementary programs check your spelling at lightning computer speeds. Computerized thesauruses help you select the best words to express your precise thoughts. Grammar-checking programs review what you have written and help you to observe the myriad of proven English grammar rules you once knew, but that are now hidden deep in your subconscious.

However, in spite of all these incredible advances in personal computers, one vital aspect of writing has been sorely neglected: the development of new techniques to help a writer enhance the *creative* aspects of his or her profession. These missing creative aspects are to originate, research, evaluate, and organize the diverse material that forms the solid foundation for your writing. This book is dedicated to those indispensable elements of writing, and introduces a unique concept that is an ideal complement to the automated computer programs that now enhance writing. I have named this new concept "modular writing."

Modular writing profits from the creations of the geniuses who developed personal computers, making available to each individual writer the full and awesome power of these modern digital marvels. Over the past few years computer sages have continually improved the word processor, the writer's best friend, adding more and more power to this fascinating computer program, taking much of the drudgery out of writing.

So what could be more logical than to utilize other related techniques devised by these computer professionals to assist and augment the creating and organizing parts of writing?

What is modular writing?

Modular writing is the technique of dividing a writing project—whether it's a memo, a report, a short story, an article, a novel, or a non-fiction book—into small, easily manageable modules.

For fiction, a module is defined as a scene or a sequel, a major division of a short story or a novel. For nonfiction, a module is defined as a major section of a chapter of a book, or a major section of an article.

A new organizing technique, the Precedent Sort is the procedure that makes modular writing possible. Modular writing and the Precedent Sort combine to make both fiction and nonfiction writing easier, and they are ideal complements to all modern word processors.

Once properly outlined, each module becomes a small, easy-to-develop section that can be brainstormed, researched, and written as a self-sufficient element of writing. The individual modules can be organized with the Precedent Sort, then written in whatever order is optimum for the writer.

When all the individual modules have been completed, they can be joined together, with appropriate transitions, to create a logical, coherent, smooth-flowing, easy-to-read and easy-to-understand manuscript.

A **nonfiction module** is an entity that has a beginning, a middle, and an end. It can be researched, organized, and written largely as a stand-alone unit of writing. Nonfiction modules are usually designated by a bold heading or some other type of obvious separation, such as double spacing, numbering, etc. The module you are reading now began with the heading, 'What is modular writing?' and is concluded just before the next heading, 'Clarity results from good organization.'

A **fiction module** is defined as a scene, or a sequel (both will be described later) that can be created, researched, and written as a separate entity. It also has a beginning, a middle, and an end. The fiction module is usually designated by a physical separation between modules such as double spacing, or the start of a new chapter.

I devised modular writing by evaluating and adapting some of the key, top-down design principles used by computer professionals. Computer programmers tackle a huge programming project (such as a word-processing program) by starting at the top, defining and breaking the project down into individual, stand-alone modules, thus developing a detailed, master outline of the total program. Each computer module performs a unique and complete function.

For example, one module could be designed to position the cursor on a video screen, another module could be designed to perform automatic word-wrap, a third module could be designed to delete a character. When the code is written for all the individual modules, and they are joined together, under control of a master outline, they form a complete, integrated, and highly versatile program.

A similar procedure *can* and *should* be used for writing, whether you write a memo, a poem, an article, a novel, a report, or a nonfiction book. *Any* type of manuscript can be top-down planned and divided into easy-to-write modules.

Individual modules can then be developed and transitions created to tie all the modules together into a coherent manuscript. The master outline, the master plan that ties them all together and makes modular writing possible, is the proper *organization* of your writing.

> *"I have on my table a violin string. It is free to move*
> *in any direction I like. If I twist one end, it*
> *responds; it is free. But it is not free to sing.*
> *So I take it and fix it into my violin. I bind*
> *it and when it is bound, it is free for*
> *the first time to sing."*
> Rabindranath Tagore

That is what organization does for you. It helps you take your creative ideas, your plots, your research, the right words that alone can do nothing, then order and bind them into a clear narrative so they are free to sing your song.

Clarity results from good organization

The most important quality of all good writing is clarity. Writing is clear when your reader can understand its meaning on the first reading. And clarity results largely from the organization of your topics *before* you start writing. Thus, the most important single key to understanding written communication is good organization!

"Order is heaven's first law," said Alexander Pope. Our minds demand order, form. Your sentences, your paragraphs, your pages, your chapters may have all the facts, but their meaning may be foggy and unclear unless proper order, grouping, subordination, and logical links are present. Your reader has neither the time, nor the patience, nor probably even the knowledge to make the effort required to sort these out. That is your task as a writer.

Organizing your material is much like taking a random, meaningless jumble of words, such as:

Haverford knee the put
Duchess The on Kent's
Earl of hand of his

and organizing them into a coherent sentence:

**The Earl of Haverford put his hand
on the Duchess of Kent's knee.**

You must have a systematic, overall plan of development to transport your reader from one logical point or event to the next. This plan is the outline, the organization, the ordering of your material.

The outline breaks your mass of material down into small, manageable modules so you can achieve this logical progression.

A document, whether it's a short memo, an article, a short story, or a book that is properly researched and logically organized, is half-written. Yet, one of the most difficult tasks, most writers agree, is organizing their work.

In a comprehensive survey, more than 1,000 professionals were asked what bothered them the most about writing. Leading the list, and far ahead of the dozens of complaints, at an amazing 28 percent, was: *"organizing and outlining."*

In another survey of a group of technical writers, professionals who earn their daily living from writing, a mere five percent said they used *no* outlines for their writing. Undoubtedly the foggy writing you have suffered through while struggling with the dismal manuals accompanying your home appliances and your assemble-it-yourself purchases was written by this unorganized five percent.

Figure 1 diagrams some of the modules that will be covered in the remainder of this chapter. This is not in an outline form, but is rather a summary, a graphical representation of the logical progression of the modules.

The curse of Roman numerals

Many of you may still harbor painful memories of being forced to outline stories, articles, poems, or even books in your high school or college classes. And you were ordered to construct your outline using Roman numerals.

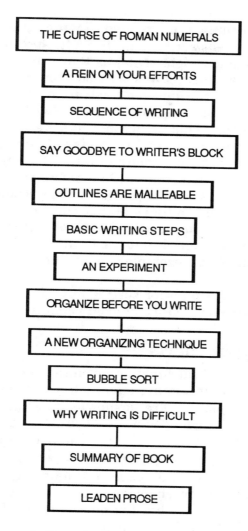

Figure 1. Organization of Chapter One Modules

This CRN (Curse of the Roman Numerals) is about to be lifted from you. Never again will you have to remember how to count, Roman style.

In this book the CRN method will be replaced by a logical, simple, easy-to-use outlining technique that *does not use a single Roman numeral!*

It was not only the dreaded Roman numerals that made outlining such a boring, difficult, and meaningless task. Another major deterrent was that you were forced to outline material *after* it was written. You were supposed to deftly remove the meager flesh from the bones of a skilled author's writing and emerge with a perfectly formed skeleton. This is wrong! It's very difficult to attempt to second-guess authors and try to divine how and why they organized their topics in a specific way.

You must complete your outline *before* you begin writing. Only in this way can you form the proper skeleton, make sure that all the limbs are assembled in the correct order, see that no unneeded joints or extra limbs are included, and be assured that the fleshed-out material will form the basis for an exemplary model of cogent and slender prose.

An outline is a plan for sorting out your thoughts and analyzing your material, *before* you begin to write.

A rein on your efforts

Another important function outlining serves is to provide a rein on your writing efforts. If you claim you can't outline your topics, you're acknowledging that you don't know what you're going to write about. If you begin writing before you know your subject, your writing can become as circuitous and as hazardous as a maze.

It's difficult to over-emphasize the usefulness and the importance of a comprehensive outline. An outline guides you in the logical, step-by-step development of your modules. An outline forces you to design, and to plan your document in detail before you write, rather than just letting it randomly accumulate as you write, whether it is fiction or nonfiction. The more time and effort you invest in creating and revising your outline and in thoroughly developing modules, the easier your writing becomes. An outline is 100 times easier to work with, to mold, to modify your ideas, to develop systematically, to review, to evaluate, to revise and to rearrange, than it is to struggle and attempt to rewrite a draft of your writing. You can easily review, spot, and correct any missing or inconsistent modules when working in an outline form. And you can spot and eliminate modules that aren't necessary.

An outline provides an excellent, easy-to-evaluate picture of the form-and-substance of your writing, and of the progression of your topics. It also gives you a visual check of the emphasis, the subordination, and the interrelationships among your modules.

Sequence of writing

Some writers, because of bad experiences with outlines in high school and college, mistakenly believe that outlines stifle creativity. But that is wrong, as you will learn from this book.

Rather than stifling creativity, a comprehensive outline *enhances* a writer's creativity through the process of modular writing. When you write the modular way, it's neither necessary, nor desirable to write your manuscript in a fixed series-sequence.

You need not start at the beginning of Module One, write all the way to the end of Module One, then go on to and write the beginning of Module Two and continue writing one module after another until you reach the end.

Instead of writing in this serial manner, you can write in the random sequence that your subconscious mind creates the ideas, writing one module at a time. The most effective approach is to research and write the chapter or module or paragraphs that you know the most about, or the module or modules that interest you the most, or those that you have the most information about, first. Then you can jump to any other module or chapter you choose, and research and write those modules, using the detailed outline as your guide.

An outline gives you the confidence that all the other modules will be included and that they will be completely covered in turn. Once entered into the computer, you can add modules to your outline, modify items, move them around and delete modules with ease. No longer must you write from the beginning to the end.

Modular writing is not limited to use with a word processor. If you utilize a typewriter, or write by hand, you can still use this productive procedure. Start with a large, loose-leaf notebook (about two inches thick). Set up several dividers and label them, one for each chapter (or one for each module for shorter works). Type out your outline and install it in the front section of your loose leaf notebook. Then, as you type or hand-write your modules or your chapters, file those pages behind the appropriate chapter or module dividers, using the detailed outline as your guideline. Skip around randomly and "write as the writing spirit moves you."

And say good-bye to writer's block

One problem that plagues both beginning and professional writers is "writer's block," a phenomenon that basically prevents a writer from exercising his or her creative writing ability. This problem is essentially a *fear of starting*, of not knowing *where* or *how* to start. Writers often have brilliant endings or creative middles in their minds, but may not have solved the beginnings, so they are unable or afraid to start.

However, modular writing helps circumvent writer's block because, even if you have only prepared a sketchy outline, you can begin by writing only those modules of the story or article that you feel are the easiest to write, the modules you have plotted or have the most information about. When you write these first modules, your subconscious mind will probably be working overtime on solving the other parts of your writing. You can then update and flesh out your outline and write the other modules in any order that is best for you.

Outlines are malleable

Once you begin putting words on paper, it's very difficult to rearrange your ideas and still maintain continuity. After a rough draft is completed, it almost sets the document's prose in concrete, requiring a jackhammer effort to revise it. A comprehensive outline not only tells you what you *know* about a subject, it also shows you what you *don't know,* and on what areas you still need to research.

The big payoff from organizing and outlining your writing comes when you use it to create an in-depth article, a lengthy story, or a full-length book. Still that doesn't mean you shouldn't invest your time wisely by organizing short letters into modules that you probably could outline in your head. Practice using the modular organizing techniques covered in this book for shorter works, too. You'll not only gain experience in using them, your short letters will be easier to write, better composed, and easier to understand.

If *you* don't understand what you're going to write about, your *reader* won't be able to understand either. A detailed outline helps define precisely what you're going to write about. You'll discover that once you organize your ideas into modules, your words, sentences, paragraphs, and pages will fall into place effortlessly. When you write, it's much easier when you know what you're going to say next.

A detailed outline makes your writing more complete because knowing that you're covering all the important points, you can momentarily set aside thinking and worrying about all the other modules. You can sharply focus and concentrate all your efforts on the specific module you're writing.

An outline also serves as a progress report to check what you have written and what you still have left to eom plete.

Basic writing steps

Two basic steps in writing, whether it's a letter, a book, an article...whatever, are:

1. Research and organize your ideas
2. Write

Many skip the first step, dive right in, and start writing. Invariably they end up thrashing about, drowning in a rambling, obtuse, turgid, circumlocutious document that is difficult to compose, and even more difficult to read and understand. All the facts may be included. Each individual sentence may make sense, but unless they're arranged in a logical order, they cannot leap out from the printed paper to create the desired picture in your readers' minds.

Good writing seldom, if ever, results from a single-step procedure. Writing is not the simple process of putting words down on paper, nor of inputting them into your word processor. Several logical steps must be followed, in the proper sequence, to create good writing.

However, our brains do not function in a logical, deductive, step-by-step, chronological, beginning-to-end order when we create something. Our minds leap about, generating random thoughts, loosely connected by creative, inexplicable, associative, magical, mental machinations. Each individual thought generated may be a brilliant idea by itself, but unless we string these thoughts together in some logical, orderly pattern, like beads on a string, the result is a mindless jumble to others.

Try this experiment

To demonstrate this phenomenon, try this experiment. Relax in a comfortable chair, with a pad of paper and a pen, or in front of your word processor. Write everything down, every thought that comes into your mind for about five or 10 minutes. Then read it back and see how your mind skipped wildly about as one thought led to another related thought.

See how little sense the unorganized sequence of your thoughts would make to some complete stranger trying to read and understand what you created. No beginning-to-end order, no logic exists in your unorganized thoughts. No satisfying progression, no conclusion results. That is precisely why your readers won't be able to understand what you've written, unless you devote the requisite time to organize your material first.

A method is required to help you organize your random creative thoughts into some logical order that will make sense to your readers. This order must be established before you start to write.

Organize before you write

In summary, proper organization of your material *before* you write:

- Makes modular writing possible.
- Helps you relate and properly emphasize modules.
- Gives direction to your writing so it won't wander and helps you to compose a smooth-flowing document.
- Serves as a check to make sure that you include all the ideas you want to cover in a logical, unified, and complete sequence.
- Makes your writing easier-to-write and easier-to-read.
- Lets you concentrate on writing any module in your outline without being distracted by worrying about the other modules.

A good outline is a strong skeleton that can be expanded with additional explanations, examples, and proofs to create a well-formed, complete body. If the skeleton is not assembled and fleshed-out properly, the body will not operate smoothly, but will function in jerky, disconnected movements.

Most outlining techniques you've used before gave you much confusing theory, but very little practical help with this vital task. You've probably wrestled with the Inverted Pyramid, the Suspense Formula, Roman numerals, ad nauseam. But no technique has provided you with a simple way to organize and assemble your raw material...until now.

A *new* organizing technique

When computers were first developed, little order existed among the many methods of programming these electronic marvels. Each programmer devised his or her own technique. Each programmer wrote computer code, debugged it, revised it, debugged it again and again until the program finally worked, after a fashion. Often there were hidden "bugs" that prevented the computer from performing all of its intended functions. These bugs didn't show up until after the software was delivered and in use. The resultant "spaghetti coding" lacked logic, had no particular order, and was as scrambled as a plate of spaghetti.

However, as programs grew in complexity, and as more and more money and time were wasted in attempting to unravel the intertwined coding to make required changes, forward-looking people in the computer profession decided to establish order in this programming chaos.

A major result of these extensive computer development efforts, starting around 1970, was "Top-Down" or "Structured" programming, that is: planning, segmenting, organizing, and modularizing a program in minute detail *before* writing the detailed programming codes. As a result of these innovative techniques, programmers soon learned to live by an important aphorism, "The sooner one starts writing code (without proper top-down organization), the longer it will take to finish the program."

The same situation exists in all types of writing. The sooner you sit down and begin to write (without proper organization), the longer it will take to revise and unravel the spaghetti paragraphs and phrases you have written.

During the past 25 years, I've devoted considerable time and effort in researching, developing, and testing various methods of organizing writing. Having extensive experience in basic research and engineering development, and in most types of writing, I concentrated on developing logical methods to achieve order out of writing chaos. During this period I wrote and had published five nonfiction books, hundreds of proposals and manuals, plus many short stories and articles, so I had ample opportunity to experiment with, and evaluate various methods. I also accomplished considerable computer programming during the past 10 years. When working in both of these seemingly diverse professions, I discovered a high degree of similarity between the two, then concentrated my efforts on adapting some of the emerging and highly innovative computer programming techniques for application in fiction and nonfiction writing.

Bubble sort

To implement the process of organizing modular writing, I considered adapting the "bubble sort" computer sorting technique. After considerable experimentation, I revised and modified the basic principles of the bubble sort, finding this versatile procedure ideal for organizing a random group of related, diverse writing topics into a logical order. I named this new technique for organizing writing the "Precedent Sort (P-Sort)."

The Precedent Sort, which you will learn in this book, puts order and logic into the task of outlining. The P-Sort breaks a complex organizing task down into a series of simple, easy-to-make, one-on-one decisions. The P-Sort shows you how to compare topics, one pair at a time, and decide which has precedence: that is, which topic should be covered earlier in your document. You continue until you have made all possible comparisons and *voilà!* Your organization is complete.

Why writing is difficult

Two of the biggest problems facing writers are:

1. What to write first, and
2. What to write next.

The big, blank page staring up at you can paralyze even the most confident writer. Then, even though you

bravely break through this initial barrier and write
something down, you panic about what to write next, and
next, and next...

In spite of these psychological barriers, writers' minds
explode with ideas. However, creative ideas come to people
in a random order, bursting into one's consciousness like
kernels of popcorn exploding in hot oil.

This cacophony of inspiration pops up idea after idea,
creative ideas seemingly unrelated to each other, but
dictated by the complex interrelationships of writers' personal loves, hates, fears, worries, and experiences of all
types, and their unique educational, cultural, economic,
and ethnic backgrounds.

So the problem is not *how* to come up with ideas, but
how to evaluate them, sort them out and *organize them in
some meaningful order into modules.*

One of the main thrusts of this book is to show how to
create, sort out, evaluate, and organize your ideas into a
comprehensive, modular outline so your writing becomes
cogent, lucid and logical. Any piece of writing, whether
it's a short memo or a long novel, deserves an outline. The
length and detail required of such an outline is directly
related to the length and complexity of the subject being
covered.

Summary of book

Figure 2 diagrams, in brief summary form, the logical, step-by-step sequence the chapters this book covers to
show you how to progress from being a creator of inge-
nious ideas, through all the steps required to become a
writer who can transfer these ideas into writing that
readers can easily understand, learn from, and enjoy.

Chapter 2 covers the basic methods of organizing raw
material to make writing and reading easier. You'll learn
in Chapter 3 how to use the Precedent Sort, a unique
technique that will revolutionize the manner in which you
organize your material for all types of writing.

Next, Chapter 4 covers two practical examples that
illustrate how to use the Precedent Sort to order informa-

tion to be covered. One example covers fiction, the other example covers nonfiction.

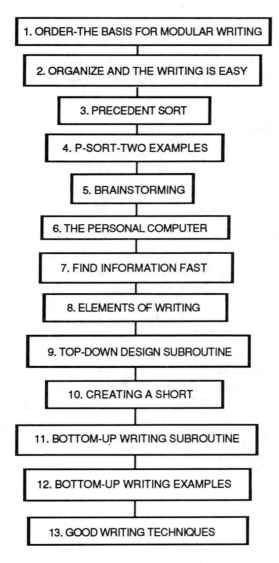

Figure 2. Organization of This Book

Chapter 5 discusses brainstorming: that is, using your inherent creativity to research and generate the basic raw material needed for a manuscript. Included are an in-depth discussion of the vital creative process, the techniques that make for improved creativity, and how to brainstorm effectively.

The enormous impact of personal computers on writing is covered in Chapter 6. The discussion covers the basic features a quality word processing program should have for a writer.

Researching your ideas

Not only do you as a writer need to create your own unique ideas, you also have to review and learn from the writings and ideas of others. As Voltaire so aptly phrased it:

"Originality is nothing but judicious imitation. The most original writers borrowed one from another. The instruction we find in books is like fire. We fetch it from our neighbor's, kindle it at home, communicate it to others, and it becomes the property of all."

Chapter 7 shows you how accomplish this "judicious imitation," borrowing from the fires of others, finding information by researching the literature. Effective use of the library, determining which reference books are the most helpful for your modules, and efficient methods for taking notes are also covered in this chapter. "Online Systems," the "Electronic Libraries of the Future," are also covered in Chapter 7.

The Magic Three

The creative part of writing is the plot, the outline, what you put into your writing, and how you order it. For the next logical step in writing techniques, the Magic Three are introduced in Chapter 8. These three magic components are the Introduction, the Body and the Conclusion.

Chapter 9 describes a universal Top-Down Planning subroutine for designing or plotting an entire manuscript by organizing the ideas created using the brainstorming techniques of Chapter 5 and the literature research of Chapter 7. Chapter 9 also shows how to "divide and conquer," taking the mountain of accumulated research material, notes, thoughts, and ideas and categorizing this raw material. Techniques illustrate how to order and subordinate topics within each individual module. The result from the procedures taught in this chapter is a detailed outline of a manuscript.

Next, Chapter 10 covers the detailed step-by-step procedures required to brainstorm, research and organize a "short." I define a short as a brief manuscript, such as a short story, an article, a report, etc. Outlines for an original short story and for an original article result from the examples demonstrated in this chapter.

The bottom-up writing subroutine for a short is covered in detail in Chapter 11. This subroutine is valid for any type of short and shows how to write a manuscript using the top-down designed outline. In Chapter 12, the outlines developed in Chapter 10 are expanded to write a sample module for both the short story and article of Chapter 10, using the bottom-up writing subroutine described in Chapter 11.

Chapter 13 covers the subject of good writing. Using well-proven techniques that are "invisible" to the reader, good writing is writing that communicates information to the reader with a minimum of effort on the reader's part. This informative chapter shows how to achieve this invisibility.

Leaden prose

To illustrate how leaden prose can become, even in everyday life, consider this jewel:

"In accordance with our previous agreement, it is hereby requested that you cease delivery from the period beginning Tuesday, May 19, up to, but not including Thursday, May 21, and that you resume, per our original agreement, on Thursday, May 21, and thereafter, until you receive further written notice from the undersigned."

This was a note to a milkman, written by an addled government bureaucrat, that should have read:

"Please skip Wednesday."

Which version would you prefer to write, and to read? This book teaches you how to remove thy lead from thy prose.

Now, after you complete the following exercises, we'll review the fundamentals of which specific ordering sequences to use when creating an outline.

Exercises

1. Which of the major literary forms are you most interested in? Articles, short stories, reports, novels, nonfiction books, or other?
2. List in a sentence or two at least one idea you have, or can create, for each of the above literary forms.
3. Conduct the experiment described in this chapter by relaxing in a chair with a pad and pencil or in front of your word processor. Let your mind free-wheel and write down *every* thought that occurs to you. Continue this exercise for five to ten minutes, then read back what you have written. Did it have any order? Would it make sense to a stranger reading what you wrote down? How many different topics did you cover? Can you find a thread, a theme, some logic that ties all of your thoughts together?

Chapter 2

Organize and the Writing is Easy

"If a man can group his ideas, he is a good writer."
Robert Louis Stevenson

Once upon a time, many years ago, in the land of the Vikings, King Thorval built a beautiful castle on the top of a high mountain. As the Norwegian king looked out over his kingdom, he saw nestled deep down in the valley a beautiful, sparkling lake. He knew he must have that sky-blue lake nearby to beautify his palace grounds for his family and his subjects, so he called in all his advisers and told them to come up with solutions to move the lake up to his castle. A huge reward awaited anyone who could solve the problem.

The king's engineers stepped forward first, confident they could accomplish the move. Hurrying down the mountainside, the engineers measured the circumference, drove stakes in the ground all around the outside of the lake and tied thick ropes to the stakes. Next they hitched a hundred oxen up to the ropes. The oxen tugged and pulled and struggled mightily to move the entire lake up the side of the high mountain, but the ropes kept breaking and the lake refused to budge. The engineers finally quit and said it couldn't be done.

Next the wise men, full of ideas and good intentions, stepped forward and boasted they could easily accomplish the feat. The wise men calculated the elevating forces needed to lift the lake, they computed the friction coefficient, factored in the slope of the mountainside, calculated day after day. But their computing, thinking, and talking totally exhausted them. They finally shook their heads and concluded it was absolutely impossible to move the lake.

Some time later Peder Espeseth, a wandering troubadour from the Far North of Norway, came to the palace to entertain the king. After the troubadour had sung a few songs, the unhappy king told the young man about the beautiful lake and the failure of his advisers to relocate it. As Peder strummed his next song, his mind raced to find a solution. Finally, as he played the last notes on his instrument, Peder lifted his head, smiled, and cried out, "It's simple!"

No one was quite sure what he meant by that, but the king called all the people in his kingdom together to hear the young man's plans. Peder composed a special song describing his idea and sang it for them. The words of the song asked all the king's subjects to make one trip to the lake each day and each time carry one full bucket of water back to the palace grounds. It was a simple solution and before long the beautiful lake glistened alongside the palace. Peder was rewarded with an appointment to be the chief adviser to King Thorval.

Writing must be planned

Writing an article, a short story, a novel or a nonfiction book is a project much like that of moving the lake to the palace grounds. It's much too big a job to jump into without planning. It's much too practical a job to only think about. Yet, if you reduce it to a detailed and well-thought-out plan, to a series of small steps, and accomplish each of these steps, one at a time, a big job can be done by even a small person. *All* big things are made up of *little* things.

That is precisely what a good outline, a logical ordering of your topics and ideas, accomplishes for you. Proper organization reduces a huge, seemingly insurmountable project into a series of small, easily manageable, interrelated modules, each of which can be completed, one at a time, and joined together until the total writing project is accomplished.

Steps required to organize

Proper organization of the material you accumulate for your writing project requires two interrelated steps:

1. Categorization
2. Ordering

Categorization consists of sorting your topics, your notes, and your research material into separate chapters and modules where the materials in each chapter and module are closely related.

The next step, **ordering**, consists of organizing the notes and research material within each category into some logical sequential order, such as chronological, spatial, cause-to-effect, etc. The end-result of these two steps is the detailed outline you can use to guide your writing.

Ordering of your material will be illustrated with examples using the Precedent Sort and will be covered in Chapters 3 and 4. Categorization of material, which covers the overall, detailed organization of a large document, follows the chapters describing research, brainstorming, and creativity.

To better understand the operation of the Precedent Sort, let's first discuss some of the basic characteristics of outlines, plus the various ordering sequences used to organize outlines.

Topic outlines vs. sentence outlines

Two basic types of outline forms are commonly used:

1. Topic
2. Sentence

A **topic outline** is an abbreviated outline that simply lists the topics to be covered in each specific part of a manuscript. A topic outline can be used when the specific meaning of each topic is clearly understood. Figure 1 of Chapter 1 is a topic outline. Here's another topic outline that lists simple headings:

- Current publishing programs
- Impact of the computer
- Future of publishing

However, a more detailed **sentence outline** should be used when a specific definition of each topic is needed. For example, the above topics could be expanded as follows:

- Description of current publishing programs. Type of equipment used, costs of publishing, elapsed time from idea to printed paper, number of copies to sell to make a profit.
- How the computer is changing publishing. Writers now submit soft copy on diskette as well as hard copy.
- Will paper copy disappear? Will all future writing be distributed via computers and data-banks, and to home TVs via fiber optic cable? How will this change the lives and livelihoods of writers in the future?

The expanded sentence outline clarifies the individual topics, making writing easier and faster. Often the sentences in a sentence outline can form the logical topic sentences for paragraphs, serving as key statements for entire strings of paragraphs. A sentence outline provides a detailed summary of what is to be written.

Both topic outlines and sentence outlines can be inter-mixed effectively when developing an outline.

Ordering patterns

"...the arrangement of words—the music of
rational speech which is in man inborn,
which appeals not to the ear only,
but to the mind itself."
Longinus

Before beginning to organize your work, select the type(s) of ordering sequence(s) you'll use to organize your topics. Material can be sequenced in three major organizational patterns:

- Natural
- Logical
- Psychological

In the **natural** order, the organization already exists and is inherent in the subject. Types of natural orders are:

- Chronological (time)
- Spatial (geographic)
- Major division
- Numerical/Alphabetical

For the **logical** order, the organization is **created by** and **imposed by** the writer and is based on inference or reason. Types of logical ordering sequences are:

- Cause to effect (problem-solution)
- Comparison-contrast
- Increasing-to-decreasing
- Specific-to-general
- Pro/con

The **psychological** order is created and used by a writer to meet the needs (emotions) of the reader. Types of psychological ordering sequences are:

- Climactic (suspense)
- How-to (combination of time and space)
- Known-to-unknown (analogy)

Orders are reversible

Note that most orders are reversible. Each of the following orders will be discussed in upcoming text, along with examples of each. All three major patterns can be

effectively intermixed, but only in different modules of the
same manuscript.

- Near-to-far or far-to-near
- Increasing size to decreasing size or vice versa
- Cause-to-effect or effect-to-cause

Natural order

A **chronologically ordered** outline arranges the topics
by the time sequence in which they occurred, or should
occur:

- Dawn
- Later that morning
- At breakfast
- At work
- The next evening

Human psychology is such that we find it easier to
understand writing that follows a common sequence,
such as time or place, as these orders are an intimate part
of our everyday lives.

You write about the first event or the topic that
occurred or should occur first, then the second in time
sequence, etc., until you have reached the last event or
topic.

Most fiction uses a chronological order, often inter-
spersing flashbacks and flashforwards. A chronological
outline is also suitable for trip reports and operating
instructions.

However, one problem inherent in a chronological
order is that it mixes together both big and little events
without proper subordination. Often you may be tempted to
include insignificant and unimportant events merely for
the sake of completeness.

The **spatial** order arranges topics in a geographical or
physical position order. This effective order is used to
describe a person, a building, a flower garden, a

manufacturing assembly line, etc. Take a look at the following example:

- Minnesota
  - Erskine
  - St. Paul
- Iowa
  - Ames
  - Decorah
- Indiana
  - Indianapolis
  - New Albany

You can go from north to south, or start at the center and move out, or go from the top to the bottom, or from left to right...the list goes on.

The **major division** order is used for topics that logically divide into natural and obvious parts. For example, a lab report is often divided into the specific major steps performed:

- Abstract
- Materials/Equipment required
  - Chemical
  - Electronic
- Test Procedures
- Results
- Conclusions

A **numerical/alphabetical** order is used to organize topics numerically or alphabetically, or when a number of arbitrary topics are to be tied together and for which no logical order or form exists.

These topics can be ordered and listed using numbers or letters, along with the topic titles, to provide some semblance of organization and to refer to in documentation. The following is an example using subjects to be discussed in an upcoming staff meeting. They are alphabetized and listed numerically:

1. Company cars—personal use
2. Moving plant to new location
3. Pay raises
4. Production problems

Logical orders

Cause-to-effect (problem/solution) or **effect-to-cause** orders cover the cause(s) that resulted in a given effect(s) or vice versa. The **cause-to-effect order** explains why something happened, or predicts what might happen as a result of the cause:

- Speeding leads to dangerous situations which leads to
- An accident which leads to
- Injury which leads to
- Crippling which leads to...

Another example:

- Unorganized sales material leads to writing that is difficult to understand, which leads to
- Reader confusion, which leads to
- Lost sales, which leads to
- Loss of jobs, which leads to...

The **effect-to-cause** order starts with the effect (a problem, a condition), then works backwards to discuss what might have caused that effect (result).
For example:

- Accident results from improper bicycle maintenance
- Flooding results from heavy rain and no preventive measures

For multiple causes and effects (either or both may be plural), an effective technique is to arrange the causes in order of increasing importance so that the first and most important cause is last and remains dominant in the reader's mind when he or she begins to read the effects.

Comparison/Contrast order compares two or more ideas or items and is sometimes linked up with advantages or disadvantages. This order can be used to compare a company's products or services to those of one or more competitors. Or it can be used to compare leasing versus purchase costs, etc. Usually you'll conclude by making one or more specific recommendations.

Our Product	**Competitor's Product**
More compact	50 percent more volume
Less costly	Cost 10 percent more
Long life warranty	Longevity not guaranteed

Topics can be arranged in order of **increasing or decreasing importance** (for example, size, value, weight, complexity, emotional impact), depending on the desired effect.

An order of **increasing importance** (also called the order of **climax**) can hold a reader's attention if the material is of sufficient interest at the beginning. As an example of increasing importance, a physician could discuss a series of potential treatments for a specific malady, starting out with the least effective technique, then working up to, and concluding with, the treatment he or she feels is best.

Conversely, an order of **decreasing importance** places the most important facts or data first to provide the reader with a quick review of the key points, then continues down the importance ladder to the bottom rung, the least important. To use this technique, a physician would start out with what he or she considers the most effective treatment for a disease, then utilize the rest of the report to explain why he or she eliminated the lesser and lesser effective treatments. This order is also effective in providing an executive summary of the most important points at the beginning of a document, then progressing to lesser and lesser important details.

An order of **increasing detail** is used in newspaper stories. In a newspaper column an entire event or topic is often summarized in the first paragraph. Subsequent paragraphs add more and more detail until the writer runs out of facts, or the editor runs out of patience or space and limits the column inches allocated. A news story has to be written in that manner so that an editor can snip the article off after any paragraph, have the article still seem complete, fit the allotted space, and still contain the gist of the story.

This order of increasing detail can be used when presenting information to a wide variety of readers, such as describing a new medicine to a lay audience and physicians. Some readers will only read the summary or introductory paragraphs at the beginning. Others interested in greater depth may read most or all of the document.

The **specific-to-general and general-to-specific** orders proceed from the little picture to the big picture, or vice versa. An example of a general-to-specific order: "Love" is a general statement. "Love of a woman" is specific, and "Love of Dorrie" is the most specific.

Specific to general

The **specific-to-general** order (also called the **inductive** order) starts with the facts, the specifics. These facts are then discussed in a logical order and used to build up to the conclusion the writer desires to prove. As an example, an industry's promotional brochure could begin by listing all the awards that company personnel have received for excellent service for one specific product. Then it could state that the same team of qualified and experienced service personnel will be servicing all of their new products, so customers can expect to receive the same, continued excellent service for future programs.

For the **general-to-the-specific** order (also called the **deductive** order), the procedure is reversed, beginning with a general statement, then adding fact after fact to justify and amplify the original statement. For example, a sales brochure could begin by stating that a company's dental services are superior to all others, then follow up with fact after fact, citing customers' satisfaction, the up-to-date automation of their services, the many advantages they offer over their competitors. By the end of the document, the weight of evidence should add up to prove the initial assertion.

Pro/con order is used to convey negative or controversial information, while still maintaining a reader's goodwill:

American view ------>   UnAmerican view

Left perspective ------>   Right perspective

For this order, both sides of a controversial question are presented: the pro and the con. The strategy is to conclude the argument with a positive statement, because that's the last thing your reader will see and hopefully remember the most. Or you can just present your evidence and let the reader draw his or her own conclusions, based on the evidence presented.

Psychological order

The **climactic** or **suspense** order sequentially reveals a little more information at a time and builds the suspense up slowly to a hopefully unexpected and entertaining climax at the end of the document. Mysteries in fiction and humor in nonfiction use this order effectively.

The **how-to-do-it** order of organizing is sometimes called the **operational** order. This order is usually a combination of time and space. The how-to is frequently used in instructional material, lectures, textbooks, recipes, tutorials, in much of the material in this book, and in how-to books. This order presents the information in the sequence the reader needs to follow to be able to understand and use the material.

Another how-to-do-it example is a procedure that arranges the steps that must be performed in a sequence to assemble (or disassemble) an object, or the steps required to perform a series of tests, or to conduct an operation or procedure, such as:

1. Open the book
2. Review Table of Contents
3. Read Chapter 1
4. Answer exercises at end of Chapter 1.

The **known-to-unknown** (or **analogy**) order is used in documents, such as instruction manuals, to explain a new equipment or theory of operation. This order is also known as the "professorial" or "teaching" method.

The writer begins with one or more facts the reader understands, then bridges to another fact that can be deduced from the first, and keeps bridging from one fact to another until the reader is informed of, and understands the unknown. As an example of this order, the flow of electricity in a wire is often compared to a phenomenon everyone is familiar with: the flow of pressurized water in a pipe.

- Water pressure is equivalent to electrical voltage
- Rate of water flow is equivalent to electrical current

Which order should be used?

Depending on the purpose of each specific part of the manuscript you are writing, you can organize your material in one or more of these specific orders:

To Explain or to get understanding
Known-to-Unknown
Comparison/Contrast
Cause-to-Effect

To Inform or to document or to entertain
Chronological
Spatial
Major divisions
Specific-to-general
Increasing or decreasing importance
How to do it
Climactic or suspense
Numerical/alphabetical

To Convince or to get action
Pro/con

In the next chapter the Precedent Sort will show you a unique and powerful technique for organizing your material. This versatile technique is one that will change your attitude about outlining forever. You can use this method for organizing a book, a chapter, an article, a manual, a report, a short story, or a novel. It's a technique that promises to revolutionize your writing.

Exercises

1. List three examples of subjects or topics that might effectively be covered in a Natural Order.
2. List three examples of subjects or topics that might effectively be covered in a Logical Order.
3. List three examples of subjects or topics that might effectively be covered in a Psychological Order.
4. Choose one of the orders listed in this chapter. Create at least eight topics or events and write them down on 3-by-5 cards. Organize the cards in the order you have chosen.
5. For Question 4, how long did it take to create this order? Are you confident that you have organized the topics properly?

Chapter 3

The P-Sort:
A New Way
to Organize

"Prose—words in their best order."
Samuel Taylor Coleridge

Your readers may be able to understand the individual words in a sentence, the specific sentences in a paragraph, but still not comprehend the meaning of the entire paragraph if the ideas, the concepts in the paragraph are not logically arranged. To be easy to understand, these thoughts must be arranged in a logical order. The new technique that simplifies the task of arranging ideas, events, thoughts, concepts, and explanations in a logical order is the "Precedent Sort." This chapter shows you how to use this revolutionary method for organizing your material, whether it's for a short or long manuscript, fiction or nonfiction, by introducing some principles and by demonstrating their use by examples.

Principle of fewness

The principle of fewness states, "The fewer items that are presented in a group, the easier it is to establish an order for that group." Utilizing this somewhat obvious, but nonetheless vital principle, the Precedent Sort reduces the size of the group to be ordered to the absolute minimum: two. It is relatively easy to compare two related topics at a time, then decide which of the two should be covered earlier in your manuscript. The principle of fewness is one of the basic principles of the Precedent Sort.

Combining the principle of fewness with the Bubble Sort of computer programming, I created the Precedent Sort, or the P-Sort, for organizing topics. The P-Sort is a step-by-step technique for sequentially comparing all the material that is to be organized. One pair of topics is compared at a time, and you decide which of the two is to be covered earlier, their order is then interchanged if needed. This comparison-by-pairs continues until all possible comparisons have been completed. The ordering or organizing of the material is then complete.

A simple example

The manner in which the P-Sort functions is best illustrated by a simple example. A series of random numbers will be used to demonstrate the mechanics and principles of the P-Sort. This first example was purposely made simple, with the choice of the precedence being obvious so you could see how the P-Sort functions without having to make subjective judgements. Chapter 4 will advance the concept more by covering two practical examples of ordering topics, one for fiction, the other for nonfiction. Both of the examples in Chapter 4 require subjective judgements.

For this first example of the P-Sort, consider this random series of numbers:

29, 7, 62, 5, 44

The P-Sort will organize these numbers in increasing numerical order by comparing two numbers at a time, then interchanging the order of the numbers so that the smaller number will always move to a more forward position. This comparison-by-pairs is to be repeated until all possible comparisons have been made.

To prepare to use the P-Sort, first record the individual numbers on five separate 3-by-5 index cards, then stack the cards in the order shown in Figure 3. Index cards are easier to handle than paper and they hold up much longer. Plus, they are ideal for manipulating when performing the P-Sort.

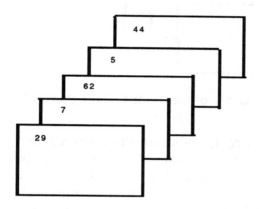

Figure 3. Initial Order of Cards

Note: The cards can be held in your hands in a one-on-top-of-the-other stack if that's more convenient. They are shown split apart in these figures simply for illustration purposes.

Enter the P-Sort

To begin, compare the first card, number 29 (see Figure 3), with the second card, number 7. Because 7 is smaller than 29, interchange the order of these two cards. The new order after the first comparison-by-pairs is shown in Figure 4.

For convenience, place the number 7 card face down and move on to make the next comparison. (Note: I haven't placed the sorted cards face down in these figures so you can better observe how the bubble sort develops after each comparison.)

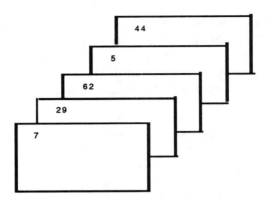

Figure 4. Order of Cards After First Comparison

Next (see Figure 4), compare the second card, number 29, with the third card, number 62. Because 29 is smaller than 62, do not interchange the order of these two cards. For now they'll remain as shown in Figure 4. Place the 29 card face down on top of the 7 card and move on to make the next comparison.Compare the third card, number 62, with the fourth card, number 5. Because 5 is smaller, interchange the order of these two cards. The new order after the third comparison by pairs is shown in Figure 5. The number 5 card can now be placed face down on top of the number 29 card.

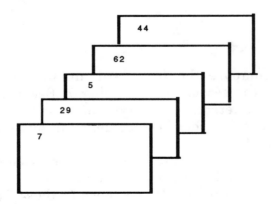

Figure 5. Order of Cards After Third Comparison

For the fourth comparison (see Figure 5), compare the fourth card, number 62 with the fifth and last card, number 44. Because 44 is a smaller number than 62, interchange the order of these last two cards. The order after the fourth comparison, the final comparison of the first round, is illustrated in Figure 6. The number 44 card can now be placed face down on top of the first three cards. Place the 62 card face up on a separate pile. The 62 card with the largest number has "sunk" to the bottom and has already been placed in its proper position.

What you have accomplished by the end of the first round of "comparisons-by-pairs" is called a "bubble sort" in computer programming. The smaller numbers are slowly "bubbling" up to the top of the pile, advancing one position forward for each round of comparisons. Conversely, the larger numbers are "sinking" to the bottom.

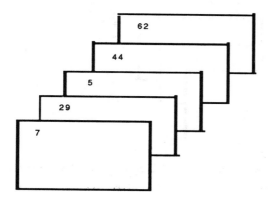

Figure 6. Order of Cards After End of First Round

Second round of comparison by pairs

To begin the second round, pick up the remaining unsorted stack of four cards (Figure 6), and compare the first two cards, number 7 and number 29. Because 7 is smaller, do not interchange their order. Again continue to place the smaller card of each comparison face down and move on to the next comparison.

For the second comparison (Figure 6), compare the second card, number 29, with the third card, number 5. Because 5 is smaller, interchange the positions of these two cards. The new order is shown in Figure 7.

For the third comparison (Figure 7), compare the third card, number 29, with the fourth card, number 44. Because 29 is smaller, do not interchange their order. Place the 44 card face up on top of the 62 card. This ends the second round of comparisons by pairs. The fourth card, 44, and fifth card, 62, have already sunk to the last positions of the order. The order after the second round of comparisons-by-pairs remains as illustrated in Figure 7.

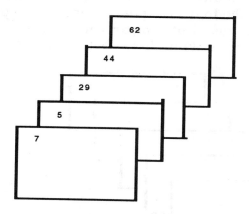

Figure 7. Order After Second Comparison, Second Round

Round three coming up

To begin round 3 (Figure 7), compare the first two cards, number 7 and number 5. Because 5 is smaller, interchange their order. The new order is shown in Figure 8.

Next, compare the third card, number 7, with the fourth card, number 29. Again 7 is a smaller number, so do not interchange their order. Place the 29 card face up on top of the 44 card. This completes round 3.

For the fourth and final round, compare the first two cards, number 5 and number 7 (see Figure 8). Because 5 is smaller, do not interchange their order. Place the 7 and 5 card on top of the 29 card. The cards have now been organized in increasing numerical order as shown in Figure 8.

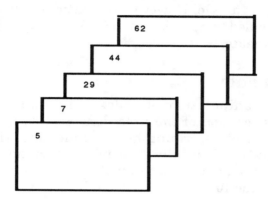

Figure 8. Order After First Comparison, Third Round

Notice that in your comparison-by-pairs, to organize five topics, you made four rounds of comparison. If you had 10 topics, you would make nine rounds of comparison. The number of rounds is always one less than the number of topics you are comparing.

At first this may seem like a laborious process just to organize five numbers in numerical order. But it was made purposely simple so that the basic idea and the mechanics of the P-Sort procedure could be better understood.

Round 1	Round 2	Round 3	Round 4
1st vs. 2nd	1st vs. 2nd	1st vs. 2nd	1st vs. 2nd
2nd vs. 3rd	2nd vs. 3rd	2nd vs. 3rd	
3rd vs. 4th	3rd vs. 4th		
4th vs. 5th			

Table 1 - Comparisons Required for Five Topics

In the next chapter, the P-Sort will be used to organize topics for both a fiction and a nonfiction manuscript. Again, because of space limitations, only five topics will be used for each example. However, the basic procedures can easily be extended to organize up to 50 to 100 topics before it becomes unwieldy.

Important note

Manual manipulation of index cards was used to explain the operation of the Precedent Sort as this is the easiest method of describing how it functions. However, the Precedent Sort is ideally suited for automation by personal computers and should be available for use with word processors in the future.

Exercises

1. If you have 10 topics to sort, how many rounds are required to sort them in **reverse** alphabetical order?
2. Write these words on individual 3-by-5 index cards and sort them in alphabetical order using the Precedent Sort:

   worm
   wallet
   corporal
   fan
   television
   fancy
   corporeal
   worse

3. By the end of the third round of Question 2, how many words had "sunk" to the bottom?
4. Shuffle the cards from Question 2 and sort the words in reverse alphabetical order.

Chapter 4

Order Out
of Chaos:
Two Examples

"Example is always more efficacious than precept."
Samuel Johnson

For these examples, I'll first illustrate the procedure I used to create and outline an article about popcorn, the all-American food. Then I'll show how to apply the Precedent Sort to fiction to create and organize an original short story I've created and entitled, "Henry."

After some preliminary research on popcorn, using the standard jump-starting questions: who, what, when, where, why, and how, and after some creative brain-storming (all will be covered in Chapter 5), I selected five modules. The identical procedures work whether there are five or 20 or 100 modules to be ordered. The five modules I chose for this example are:

1. Early history (When and Where)
2. Recipes (How)
3. Types of popcorn (What)
4. Popcorn saves movie theaters from bankruptcy (Why)
5. How to pop it (How)

P-Sort for non-fiction

To begin I wrote each module title on a separate 3-by-5 card, then stacked them in the random order shown in Figure 9.

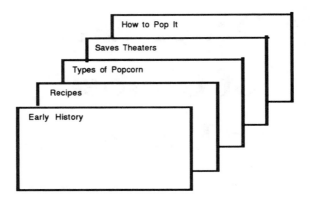

Figure 9. Initial Order of Cards

Begin comparisons

To begin the P-Sort, I compared the first and second cards of Figure 9 to decide which module should logically be covered earlier in my article. I decided that "Early history" should be covered before "Recipes," because I felt that the background history of popcorn would be an excellent way to begin an article using one or two interesting anecdotes. (Here I made a subjective decision on which module should be covered earlier.) So I did not interchange the order of the first two cards and laid the "Early History" card face down on an unsorted pile.

Next, I compared the second card in Figure 9, "Recipes" with the third card, "Types of popcorn." Logically, "Types of popcorn" should be covered before "Recipes" because the type of popcorn to be used in the recipes must be known first. So I interchanged the order of the second and third cards to the new order shown in Figure 10 and laid the "Types..." card face down on top of the "Early..." card on the unsorted pile.

For the next step, I compared the third card, "Recipes" in Figure 10 with the fourth card, "Popcorn saves theaters from bankruptcy." I elected to cover "Popcorn saves theaters from bankruptcy" first since it would seem to help build up the early part of the article with the fascinating story of how the explosive vegetable saved movie theaters from bankruptcy when television took so much business away from them. So, I interchanged the order of the third and fourth cards to that shown in Figure 11 and placed the "Popcorn saves theaters..." card face down on top of the "Types..." card on the unsorted pile.

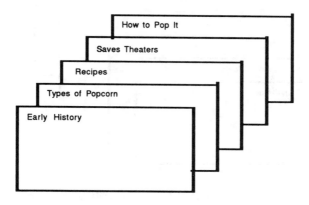

Figure 10. Order After Second Comparison

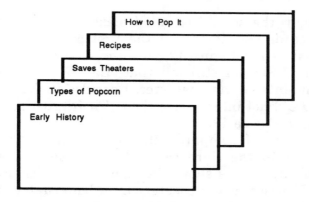

Figure 11. Order After Third Comparison

To complete the first round, I compared the fourth and fifth cards of Figure 11. "How to pop it" must come before "Recipes" since the popcorn obviously must be popped to be used in recipes, so I interchanged the order of these last two cards to that shown in Figure 12.

I then set the "Recipes" card aside, face up in a new sorted pile. The "Recipes" card, after "sinking" to the bottom, then becomes the last module to be covered in the article.

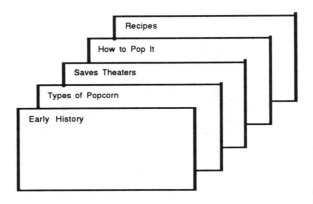

Figure 12. Order After Completion of First Round

Start of second round

To begin the second round, I picked up the unsorted stack of cards and compared the first card, "Early history," as shown in Figure 12, with the second card, "Types of popcorn." Since I still felt that "Early history" would yield some interesting anecdotes, I decided it should come first. So I did not interchange them. Their order remained as shown in Figure 12.

Continuing, I compared the second card, "Types of popcorn," with the third card, "Popcorn saves theaters from bankruptcy," as shown in Figure 12. My choice was to cover "Popcorn saves theaters from bankruptcy" before "Types of popcorn" because I felt the sale of popcorn in the theaters would be a natural interesting follow-on story to add to the early history. So I interchanged their order to that shown in Figure 13.

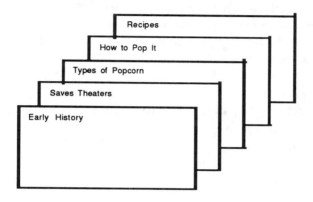

Figure 13. Order After Second Comparison, Second Round

For the third and final comparison of the second round, I compared the third and fourth cards of Figure 13. "Types of popcorn" should be covered before "How to pop it" can be discussed, so I did not interchange them. The order after the second round remained as shown in Figure 13.

Round three

To start the third round, I compared the first two cards of Figure 13. Again my decision to cover "Early History" as the first module remained firm, so I did not interchange their order. Next I compared the second and third cards of Figure 13. That concluded the third round of comparisons-by-pairs.

For the final round it was only necessary to compare the first two cards. Again "Early history" should be covered before "Popcorn saves theaters from bankruptcy," so I did not interchange their order.

In this example the modules slowly "bubbled up" to the top to take their correct sequential positions for the article. Note that although the P-Sort is a "formula," you still must make subjective judgments for each comparison, just as I had to do. Your opinion of which topic should be covered earlier may differ from mine, but that's where your individual creativity comes in. The process does indeed have room for individual opinions: That's precisely what makes it so universal in its applications.

The final order for the modules to be covered in the article then became:

1. Early history
2. Popcorn saves movie theaters from bankruptcy
3. Types of popcorn
4. How to pop it
5. Recipes

P-Sort for fiction

For the next example, I'll demonstrate the use of the P-Sort in fiction to organize and outline a short story. This original story I created will be about Henry, a middle-aged computer programmer who is taken advantage of by his shrewish wife and his dictatorial boss. To escape the "prison" he feels he is in, Henry plots to make some unauthorized electronic withdrawals and run away from his unbearable situation.

I'll use only a few major topics as some of the modules (scenes or sequels) in the story. Whether these topics will become scenes or sequels can be decided later when the complete story is plotted. These major topics or events, in the random order I conceived them, are:

• Henry plants a virus in computers to erase all traces of his crime.
• Henry sees a travel poster of an idyllic life in the South Seas that he hungers for.
• Henry pulls off his unauthorized "electronic withdrawals" caper by reprogramming the computers he works on.
• Henry ends up in the South Seas with suitcases full of money and two gorgeous, young native maidens to help him enjoy life.

- Henry is henpecked mercilessly by his wife and picked on constantly by his dictatorial boss at work.

I gave the five modules the following short titles for this example:

- Henry plants virus
- Sees travel poster
- Makes withdrawals
- Henry in South Seas
- Henry henpecked

To better follow and understand the procedure, write these five module topics down on individual 3-by-5 cards and manipulate them as directed below. These are all subjective decisions that I made. You may choose to order them in a different sequence.

Stack the cards in the order shown in Figure 14. Again, they may be held in a one-on-top-of-the-other order for convenience in handling.

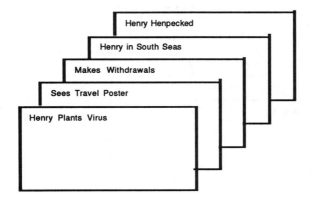

Figure 14. Initial Order of Cards

To begin, compare the first and second cards and decide which topic should logically be discussed earlier in your story. Logically "Sees travel poster" must be covered before "Henry plants virus" since the the travel poster is a motivation trigger that helps him decide to escape, to pull off his caper. So interchange the order of the first two cards to the order shown in Figure 15.

Next, compare the second card, "Henry plants virus" with the third card, "Makes withdrawals." Again Henry must make the withdrawals before he plants the virus, so interchange the order of these two cards.

Next compare the third card, "Henry plants virus," with the fourth card, "Henry in South Seas." Certainly "Henry plants virus" must be covered earlier since he has to plant the virus before he escapes to the South Seas, so do not interchange the order of these two cards.

To complete the first round, compare the fourth and fifth cards. "Henry henpecked" should certainly be covered before "Henry in South Seas," because the hen-pecking is one of the major motivating factors in his decision. So interchange the order of these last two cards. At the con-clusion of the first round of comparisons, the cards should be ordered as shown in Figure 15. So, the story will con-clude with Henry in his South Seas paradise.

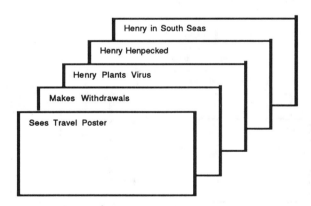

Figure 15. Order After First Round of Comparisons

To begin the second round, compare "Sees travel poster" with "Makes withdrawals." Logically the travel poster topic must come earlier, so do not interchange the order of these cards. Next, compare "Makes withdrawals" with "Henry Plants Virus." Again, "Makes withdrawals" must be covered before "Henry plants virus," so do not interchange their order.

For the third and final comparison of the second round, compare "Henry plants virus" with "Henry henpecked." "Henry henpecked" must come first as one of the major motivations for his caper, so interchange the order of these two cards. The order at the conclusion of the second round of comparisons is shown in Figure 16.

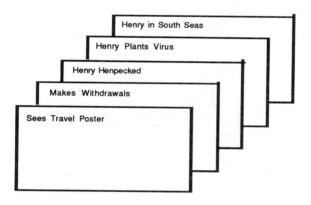

Figure 16. Order After Second Round of Comparisons

In round three, "Sees travel poster" must come before "Makes withdrawals," so do not interchange their order. Next, "Makes withdrawals" should not be covered until "Henry henpecked" has motivated Henry, so interchange the order of the second and third cards. The results at the end of the third round are shown in Figure 17.

For the final round, it is only necessary to compare the first two cards. "Henry henpecked" is a logical choice to be the first and introductory motivating topic in the short story since it sets up the rest of the scenes and sequels, so interchange the order of the first two cards. The final order accomplished by use of the Precedent Sort is shown in Figure 18. The "Henry henpecked" topic has "bubbled" to the top and has become Scene /Sequel 1.

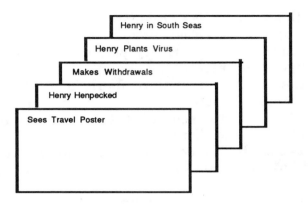

Figure 17. Order After Third Round of Comparisons

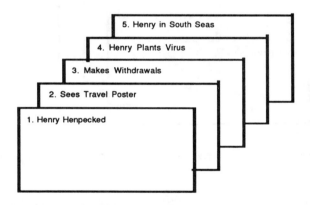

Figure 18. Final Order of Scenes/Sequels

This is an example of how I organized a short story using the P-Sort. Your choice of the sequence of scenes and sequels could be entirely different. For example, you could have decided that you would begin the story with Henry in the South Seas and then flash back to how he got there. Many other combinations are possible.

So you see that the P-Sort is not a mechanical way of organizing. It is a powerful method that helps you use your individual creativity to plot a story, a book, a speech, or whatever you want to organize in *your own way*.

The same technique can also be used to organize:

- Chapters in a novel
- Scenes and sequels within each chapter
- Chapters and modules in a nonfiction book
- Events in a novel, a report, a short story, a non-fiction book
- Modules in an article

Next?

The Precedent Sort helps you take any number of topics (you can expand the list up to 100 modules or topics before it becomes unwieldy and time-consuming) and organize them in an ordered pattern that makes your writing flow logically and easily from one module to the next.

It's much easier to don a pair of blinders, fully concentrate, eliminate the distraction of thinking about any of the other modules, and compare only two modules at a time, side-by-side, and decide which should come first, rather than befuddle the issue by attempting to compare and juggle 50 to 100 modules, in a hit-or-miss fashion.

Important guidelines to observe when using the Precedent Sort are:

1. Proceed logically from the first card to the last, in sequential order. Don't jump around or your results will not be accurate and the compar-isons-by-pairs will be confusing.

2. Don't decide that it's unimportant which mod-ule comes first and neglect to interchange the order of the cards. Make a judgement for *each* comparison. Weigh all the factors as best you can. Take all the time you need to make each comparison (minutes or hours, or even sleep on it if needed. The cards won't go anywhere until you move them). If all else fails, just guess, but you *must* make a decision or the process won't

come out right. Besides, if you don't like the final results, you can always redo the P-Sort or change the order around later.

3. Before making your comparisons-by-pairs, be sure that you understand precisely what each module is and means. This is very important. If you're not sure, write out a statement or two, a summary, or a paragraph or two on the card to define precisely what each topic or module means before you start making your comparisons. There is no length restriction on what you can write on each card. Write as much as you need to define each module *precisely* for yourself.

4. The wording on the cards need not be a few words, it can be sentences, statements, diagrams, notes, questions...whatever you need to rank, order, or outline.

A caution

Don't conclude that the P-Sort is a mechanical, robot-like method of organizing writing, because it isn't. You still must use your subjective judgement, your unique creativity just as you do when you use many "writing formulas." The P-Sort is a tool that provides the mechanics and the procedures to help break a huge, perplexing problem down into a series of simple-to-make, one-on-one, orderly, logical, individual decisions.

Other applications for the P-Sort

The Precedent Sort has many other applications:

1. Schedule tasks, to itemize the order in which jobs must be accomplished to reach an end goal in a logical, efficient manner.

2. Rank topics in a sales brochure, listing the most important features first.

3. Arrange a large group of items in either a numerical, chronological, or alphabetical order.

4. Assign jobs. Use two P-Sorts. Use one to rank your employees in order of their competence. Use a second P-Sort to rank the jobs to be done, in their order of difficulty. Finally assign your best employee to your most difficult job, your second best to the second most difficult, and so on.

5. Arrange ideas to be sold or justified in order of difficulty, such as in a proposal where you should spend the most time discussing the most difficult problems that need to be solved.

6. Break a big decision into a series of small decisions that must be settled before the big decision can be made, such as you must do when you are deciding to purchase a major item such as a car or a home.

7. Judge contests ranging from speeches (ranking the speakers for 1st, 2nd, and 3rd prizes), to cattle shows, to a cake-baking contest, to beauty contests.

Next, Chapter 5 shows you how to exercise your creativity muscles to develop the raw material for your fiction and nonfiction.

Exercises

1. List six or more topics you feel would be suitable to include in an article. Use the Precedent Sort to order these topics and to create a skeleton outline for an article.

2. List six or more events you feel would be suitable for a short story. Use the Precedent Sort to order these events to form a basic plot for your story.

Chapter 5

Brainstorming: Exercising Your Creativity

"The trick in coming up with good ideas is to think up a great many ideas and then to get rid of the bad ones."
Linus Pauling

On a bright, sunny Minnesota afternoon, two children came trudging down the street; an 8-year-old girl solicitously leading her younger brother, who had his eyes tightly shut.

A watching passerby asked, "What's the matter? Did he hurt his eyes?"

"Oh, no," was the little girl's casual reply. "We do this every Saturday when the sun's so bright. He keeps his eyes closed and I lead him to the movies. Inside the theater, he opens his eyes and finds both of us a seat in the dark."

Everyone is creative

Everyone is creative and creativity manifests itself in many different and unusual ways, as it did with that innovative little girl. It's just that some people know how to put their creativity to work, while others do not.

A team of researchers at Princeton University, investigating where new ideas come from, discovered that "creative behavior is inherent in man's nature." The researchers concluded, "Creativity is not confined to a few gifted people. As we have been able to show in our research, people can be influenced to behave in creative ways and can be *trained* to increase their creativity."

People differ only in their degree of creativity and how they utilize it. Because we learn by imitation, anyone can enhance his or her creativity by consciously cultivating and practicing some of the attributes that characterize creativity. It's not knowledge alone that makes us creative, it's what we *do* with that knowledge.

Creative people often use what is already available and change it in unconventional ways. Frequently a new idea is simply an original arrangement of old ideas. Henry Ford came up with an original arrangement of mounting an internal combustion engine on a buggy and created the automobile.

We are creative even when we relax. Psychologists have demonstrated that creative people produce more alpha waves while they are relaxing than other people. A study of 200 scientists concluded that successful hunches burst upon the scientists during a lazy period following hard work on the problems they were trying to solve.

Our subconscious minds work hard, even when we relax. That's why it's good advice to let your writing "cool" before you review and rewrite it.

Yugoslavian inventor

Nikola Tesla, a creative engineering genius, contributed much to the development and application of electricity and earned 112 U.S. patents. While employed by Westinghouse Electric, he was largely responsible for the alternating current adopted as the standard for electrical power systems. The inventions of this Yugoslavian immigrant ranged from alternating current, to radio and television, to guided missiles.

In an interview entitled, "Making Your Imagination Work For You," published in the April 21, 1921 issue of *American Magazine*, Tesla outlined his creative process:

"Some people, the moment they have a device to construct or a piece of work to perform, rush at it without adequate preparation, and immediately become engrossed in details, instead of the *central idea*. They may get results, but they sacrifice quality.

"Here, in brief, is my own method. After experiencing a desire to invent a particular thing, I may go for months or years with the idea in the back of my head. Whenever I feel like it, I roam around in my imagination and think about the problem without any deliberate concentration. This is a period of incubation.

"Then follows a period of direct effort. I choose carefully the possible solutions of the problem I am considering and gradually center my mind on a narrowed field of investigation. Now, when I am deliberately thinking of the problem in its specific features, I may begin to feel that I am going to get the solution. And the wonderful thing is that, if I do feel this way, then I know I have really solved the problem and shall get what I am after.

"The feeling is as convincing to me as though I already had solved it. I have come to the conclusion that at this stage the actual solution is in my *subconscious*, though it may be a long time before I am aware of it *consciously*.

"*Before I put a sketch on paper, the whole idea is worked out mentally*. In my mind I change the construction, make improvements, and even operate the device. Without ever having drawn a sketch, I can give the measurements of all parts to workmen, and when completed, all these parts will fit, just as certainly as though I had made the actual drawings. It is immaterial to me whether I run my machine in my mind or test it in my shop.

"The inventions I conceived in this way have always worked. In 30 years there has not been a single exception. My first electric motor, the vacuum tube wireless light, my turbine engine, and many other devices have all been developed in exactly this way."

Plan (organize) before you act

"Chance favors the prepared mind."
Louis Pasteur

Notice how Tesla cautioned against jumping in before a project was well-planned, well-thought out, well visualized (as in an outline). He said, "They may get results, but they sacrifice quality." And quality in writing is creating a logical, easy-to-understand, informative, entertaining document.

"Before I put a sketch on paper, the whole idea is worked out mentally," he also said. He was able to "change the construction, make improvements, even operate the device." That's precisely what an outline does for a writer. You can work your writing plans out mentally, change the construction, make improvements, while your ideas are still in an easily changeable, outline form. So think (plan) first and write later.

Creativity

"It's better to create than to be learned; creating is the true essence of life."
Reinhold Niebuhr

A person's creativity can be best utilized when he or she makes a concerted effort to be:

- Unconventional
- Original
- Curious
- Sensitive
- Discontented
- Open Minded
- Image Creating
- Fluent
- Persistent/Motivated
- In possession of a sense of humor

This may seem to be a large number of characteristics to have, but everyone possesses these attributes to varying degrees. The more you consciously cultivate these gifts, the more you will be able to take full advantage of your creativity.

Creativity was first manifested in us when we were children, always curious, always asking questions, always trying new things. Unfortunately this creativity was often stifled by parents, teachers, and elders who judged us harshly and impatiently, scolding us for asking such silly questions (Where does the sun go at night?), or performing such stupid antics (climbing a water tower to get a better view). All through life we have been continually judged and told not to do certain things. Some of these cautions served a useful purpose. But in many instances it probably would have been better if we had had the opportunity to learn from and suffer the consequences ourselves.

As adults we later become so conditioned to accept the status quo that we are afraid to suggest improvements for fear that our peers will judge us harshly or laugh at us. Thousands of examples exist of creative people being laughed at, from Noah, to Fulton, to modern-day researchers. But these creative people endured the criticism and carried their ideas to fruition. Much of this criticism is unwarranted and rooted in envy.

Creative urge may be dormant

"Anyone can spark an idea, but only an individual can have one. As former President Griswold of Yale has so aptly asked, Could 'Hamlet' have been written by a committee? Or the 'Mona Lisa' be painted by a club?"
W. John Upjohn

The basic creative urge is still present in all of us, lying dormant, waiting to be nourished, eager to be activated again. Curiosity is like a muscle, it must be exercised frequently to be of full use.

No one has been able to accurately define or predict creativity, it can only be judged by its results. Many creative people claim their creativity is unconscious. Ideas come from out of nowhere.

Our minds retain millions of images of what we have seen, information we have learned, ideas we have thought about. And our creative minds seem to be able to filter these out and bring them together in unusual combinations to create something new, something unique.

Unique combinations of new ideas can be triggered in many different ways. Sometimes we can read and think deeply about a problem, completely immerse ourselves in it, then set aside thinking about it for an hour, or for a few days. Then we may wake up in the middle of the night, or be in the shower, or be weeding in our garden and the solution pops into our heads.

In this book you're going to have an excellent opportunity to exercise your "creativity muscles" by putting them to work to generate the raw material for writing an article, a short story. Properly planned, a series of related articles can add up to a book and a series of chronological short stories can add up to a novel.

Ideas feed on ideas, so what may have seemed like a totally ridiculous idea can give birth to that great, earth-shaking, revolutionary idea that springs forth and that can change your life for the better.

Dare to be different

> "Daring ideas are like chessmen moved
> forward; they may be beaten, but
> they start a winning game."
> Goethe

Unconventional. Creative people employ unique problem-solving techniques and give uncommon answers to questions in the process of generating unusual solutions to problems. They balk at pressure to conform to the norm. They're not afraid to try something different, to take a chance.

Washington, D.C., with its many circular parks placed in the middle of many of its main streets, annoys some drivers as they are forced to swerve around these circles. This unique design was devised by an unconventional and creative individual. The French engineer who designed Washington, Pierre Charles L'Enfant, came up with an unusual approach after he observed the mobs of the French Revolution race unhindered through the streets of Paris. To prevent such a recurrence in the American capital city, he designed the circles in Washington, D.C., so that cannons placed in them could block entry to the city from any direction.

A creative person, such as Pierre L'Enfant, does not fit into a mold. The creative person is not necessarily the one with the best memory. Studies have shown that people with exceptional memories are not creative, but are imitative. For example, an *idiot savant* can have a photographic memory, but is in no way creative.

The basic definition of creativity is the ability to come up with something new, something different. So a truly creative person is one who thinks differently, who sees objects and situations in a different light.

Original. Creative people are always searching for something new and are not hampered by stereotyped solutions. When writing, they can create truly original descriptions of commonplace objects.

A young girl was assigned the task of defining a bolt and a nut. After studying the two, she described them in her own original way:

"A bolt is a thing like a stick of hard metal, such as iron, with a square bunch at one end and a lot of scratching around the other end. A nut is similar to the bolt, only just the opposite, being a hole in a little chunk of iron sawed off short, with wrinkles around the inside of the hole."

Truly creative people don't write clone descriptions. Their writing is original as this imaginative young girl's was. They can analyze existing writing and see room for improvement, devise alternate ways to write it. They can create unusual word combinations to arrive at a new and better description. Receptive to new ideas, they delight in rearranging basic thoughts into new combinations to form totally new entities.

Sensitive. Responding strongly to their senses of hearing, touching, tasting, and their sensitivity to color, shapes, and textures also distinguish the creative individual.

Louis Pasteur was a sensitive individual who hated to see people endure pain. As a nine-year-old, he had heard the agonized cries of a farmer who had been bitten by a rabid wolf being treated by pressing a white-hot iron to his leg. The sickening odor of sizzling flesh and the agonized screams of the man burned deeply into Pasteur's mind and the young boy ran away, crying. But the hot iron was useless against rabies and the farmer died in the horrible agony of hydrophobia. This seared a life-long hatred of pain and death in the sensitive lad. That sensitivity and hatred toward death hardened Pasteur against the sneers of the medical profession when he, only a lowly chemist, dared to promote his theory that microbes are the worst enemies of humanity. But time was to prove Pasteur's genius.

Being sensitive, creative people have a greater "feel" for things and events that surround them. They see and feel more than most people.

Curious. A predominant characteristic of creative people is that they have never totally lost their childhood wonder. They become intrigued by problems that puzzle them and ponder how these problems can be solved. They wonder about things, events, processes. What caused them? Can the results be changed? Can a process be done in a different and better way?

Chester Grummond was born curious and asked so many questions that he drove his teachers and parents to distraction. When he was 15 years old in 1873, he discovered he could keep his ears from freezing by holding his mittens to cover his ears as he braved the sub-zero temperatures of Western Maine. But he knew he looked silly as he walked and held his hands up over his ears. Curious, he thought there was a better way to keep his ears warm so he attached small, fur cups to both ends of a wire and bent the assembly to fit over his head. The first earmuffs were thus created and orders soon came in from all over the community.

Discontent. Creative people are dissatisfied with the way things are, dissatisfied enough to change them. They don't accept situations as inevitable. They are restless, yet they cherish the opportunity to relax and switch their minds over to something different. This discontent does not disturb them to the point of rejection, but to the point of wanting to improve it. They know there are better ways to accomplish things. I call it a "divine discontent."

Ole Evinrude had a sweetheart named Bess. On a hot Sunday afternoon in August, Bess said she wanted a strawberry ice cream cone. The young Evinrude left Bess at the lakeside picnic area west of Milwaukee, Wis., and hopped into a row boat. A strong youth, Ole rowed across the one-mile wide lake to an ice-cream stand and bought his girl friend a double scoop.

Hurrying back, a full ice-cream cone in one hand, the young Norwegian-American rowed as fast as he could to try to get back to the island before the sun melted the ice cream. But the sun won. By the time he returned to the picnic area, the ice cream had reverted to its original form and melted all over his arm. His friends laughed at the man with the strawberry arm.

Discontented with the slow speed of a row boat, Ole pondered how to devise a faster way to get across the lake. Working diligently, he soon created an idea for a quicker method and invented the Evinrude outboard motor. The rest is history.

Open-minded. A prime requirement of creativity is the ability to react to stimuli without prejudice, without shutting out pertinent information. Creative people react differently to unusual ideas. They give every idea a fighting chance. They are not hobbled by preconceived ideas of what will and what will not work.

When Thomas Edison was complimented as an inventive genius, he shifted on his feet and nervously cleared his throat. "Well," Edison explained, "I guess I'm an awfully good sponge. I absorb ideas from every source I can and put them to practical use. Then I improve them until they become of some value. The ideas I use are mostly the ideas of people who don't bother to develop them."

Like Edison, creative people open their minds to *all* ideas. An ability to restrain critical judgement during the early creative or idea-generation process, and an openness to all approaches, distinguishes the creative person. Creators don't necessarily believe that the obvious way is the best way. Receptive to unusual ideas and coupled with a talent for handling ambiguity, they can work in situations where no clear direction exists. Creative individuals can find their way in the dark without a candle.

> *"Imagination is the eye of the soul."*
> Joseph Joubert

Creator of Images. Creative people think in images, not in words. They tend to be day-dreamers and can visualize an idea taking shape, form, and substance. They believe it's best to solve most of the problem with images, even though their initial imagery may be foggy and ill-defined at first.

Michael Faraday, the great physicist, took a bit of steel and wire and, laboring with infinite pain, created a little, toy-like instrument. He demonstrated this to a group of men and women. One man in the audience sneered, "Of what possible use is this toy?"

"Sir," Faraday replied, drawing himself up tall. "Of what use is a new-born baby?"

The little instrument Faraday had a vision for grew up to prove the theory of electromagnetic induction, the phenomenon forming the very heart of the great commercial world of electrical generators today. Faraday didn't see the toy that he built as an end, but as a beginning. He had an image of bigger things that would result from his discoveries.

Fluent. Possessing fluency, creative individuals can generate 50 uses for a paper clip. They are fluent not only in their own field, but also in many related fields. Fertility of ideas also characterizes this type of individual. They can generate a large number of ideas in a short time. Ideas spawn other ideas, loosening the flood gates of imagination so that a large number of potential solutions will emerge. As a result of this chaining effect, an outstanding solution usually results.

Flexible. The ability to adapt and adjust to new and changing situations is also important. Creative people can abandon old ways of thinking and initiate different directions, different problem-solving approaches. They can generate a number of different kinds of ideas and are able to break away from conventional methods of solution.

Persistent/motivated. Creative people don't work an eight-hour day and they don't function to a schedule. They tend to become immersed in their work, fiercely determined to succeed. Not overly discouraged by failure, they realize that some failures, some stumbling is necessary in learning to walk the path to complete the work they have started.

One summer evening, when Thomas Edison returned home from work, his wife scolded him, "You have worked long enough without a rest. You must go on a vacation."

"But, where will I go?" he asked, puzzled.

"Decide where you would rather be than anywhere else on earth and go there." she replied.

"Very well," Edison replied. "I will go there tomorrow."

The next morning Thomas Edison returned to his laboratory.

A strong drive is probably the most important characteristic of creative people. More energetic, they have a strong desire to create and they welcome confrontation. They are not discouraged by the unknown, they accept it as a challenge. Creative people have a huge capacity to take pains. They are stubborn, determined to see their project through to completion.

Sense of humor. The great satirist George Orwell said, "Every joke is a tiny act of rebellion." This rebellion is characterized in creative individuals by their ability to laugh at life's foibles, incongruities.

Mozart was a person who could create a musical joke when the occasion motivated it. Mozart hoodwinked his friend, Haydn, with a piece he had just written. Mozart dared Haydn to play it, and as Haydn tried it out on the harpsichord, he was stopped cold at a certain passage. On the manuscript Mozart had inserted a note to be struck in the center of the keyboard at precisely the same time the right hand was playing in high treble and the left hand in low bass. Haydn indignantly declared nobody could possibly execute that passage because it necessitated the use of a third hand. With a twinkle in his eye, Mozart sat on the harpsichord bench. As he reached the crucial part of the composition, Mozart bent over and struck the central note with his nose.

Humor and creativity go hand in hand. Some experts maintain that computers will never be able to do creative thinking because computers have no sense of humor. But it is a healthy, positive sense of humor that creative people possess, not a destructive, negative, degrading, cynical one.

Now it's time to put your creativity to work. And one of the best methods to exercise it is *brainstorming*.

Brainstorming

Brainstorming is a process in which you think about your subject *uncritically*, without giving any thought to organization, nor of judging an idea's worth. You open the floodgates of your mind and write down every idea you have about your subject, in whatever random order it occurs to you. You are "writing your mind" as your thoughts occur. You should let the ideas gush out in any form, in any sequence. Don't attempt to evaluate your material at this point. Even if it might be an idea you've written down before, write it down again: You may rephrase the idea better. Creative thinking requires a positive attitude, so write down *all* of your ideas, knowing for certain that some of them will be good.

When brainstorming, you're actually writing for discovery. You are discovering new thoughts, new concepts by exploring, imagining, pondering, testing, experimenting with new approaches, speculating, suspending doubt, delving into new areas of thought and new experiences.

Critically judging your ideas too early is the biggest single enemy of brainstorming and must be avoided, or it may cut off the flow of ideas. Or you may disregard some promising ideas. You can produce 10 times as many ideas freewheeling than you could if you pause to judge each one when it occurs to you. Defer your judgement until later or you may critically evaluate and discard ideas that may not initially seem good, but which, through association with **other** ideas, could give birth to **new** ideas. Many of your attempts at coming up with new ideas may be pure garbage. But a precious few of them can be diamonds.

Remember, you can critically evaluate and organize your ideas later. To brainstorm effectively, your brain must roam free, unorganized, unfettered, unbiased, uncensored.

Psychologists have observed that very creative people are more distupbed by loud, jarring noises than other people are. To get ready for your brainstorming session, find a quiet place, one free of distracting noises.

To begin your brainstorming session, get a supply of blank note cards (3 by 5 or whatever size you prefer). If you already have some note cards on your subject, begin by reading through those note cards and let your mind do a little creative wandering as you read them.

If you haven't made any notes yet, start making some on these blank cards. Don't worry about spelling, grammar, or punctuation. Write down a title, the subject, anything you can think of about your topic. Use incomplete sentences, phrases, ideas. This is necessary to jump-start your brain. This warming-up process activates your mental muscles, setting the marvelous process of idea association to work. Our brain tends to file all information it receives in an associative manner.

Each time you read one of your note cards, or write down a note, one or two more associated ideas or thoughts will pop into your mind. Quickly jot them down on separate blank cards, one idea, one thought per card. A huge quantity of ideas is needed. Quantity helps breed quality. Build new ideas and modify the ideas you've already written down. Write all your thoughts down, no matter how wild and impractical they may seem. You are writing these down for only yourself to see, so don't be embarrassed by what you write.

Brainstorming with a PC

One of the advantages of using a word processing program in your personal computer is that it's so easy to stop and make corrections on the screen. But this feature can be a distinct disadvantage when using a PC to brainstorm. Because it's so easy to edit as you input, to pause and correct a misspelling or to restructure a sentence, many writers find that this immediate editing kills their creative juices.

However, there is a method you can use to brainstorm effectively with a PC. After you've turned your computer on and are in your word processing program, turn the brightness down so low that the monitor screen is blank. Then you can brainstorm about whatever topics you want by inputting words, phrases, stream-of-consciousness writing...without being able to correct on the screen. Forget about misspelled words, improper sentence construction. The PC's memory will store everything you have written and save it for later recall and review.

After 10 to 20 minutes, or perhaps longer, your creative juices may run dry. But the computer has remembered **everything** you have input, so you can then save it in an idea file, run off a printed copy to review at your leisure, and select the few roses out of the weeds for use in your writing.

Six honest serving men
"I keep six honest serving men
(They taught me all I know);-
Their names are What and Why and When
And How and Where and Who."
Rudyard Kipling

One of the most effective ways of using brainstorming to explore and expand on a subject, is using the six honest serving men that taught Kipling all he knew. These six honest serving men that function as jump-starters for brainstorming are:

- What?
- Why?
- When?
- Where?
- Who?
- How?

Although this brainstorming method may not give you many answers, it usually gives you many pertinent questions that you may need to research. To use this technique, take a few sheets of paper and list at the top of each sheet one of the six key queries listed above. Then let your mind wander and list all you can think about your subject on the appropriate sheet.

For fiction you can vary the six queries to ask the following questions:

- What if he or she or it ....?
- Why did he or she or it ....?
- When did he or she or it ......?
- Where did he or she or it .....?
- Who did he or she or it ....?
- How did he or she or it.........?

To illustrate its use in nonfiction, I'll summarize some of the brainstorming I did for another article on popcorn.

What?
What kinds (varieties) of popcorn are available?
What quantity of popcorn is used per capita?
What kind of popcorn popper is best (hot oil, hot air, microwave)?

What kinds of popcorn are the best (by types or brand names)?
What's the best way to serve popcorn?
What are "old maids" and "grannies" in popcorn lingo?

Why?
Why is popcorn so popular?
Why does popcorn pop?

When?
When was popcorn first discovered?
When do people eat the most popcorn at the movies?
When did the American Indians introduce popcorn to the American colonists?

Where?
Where is popcorn grown?
Where in the world (what countries) do people eat and enjoy popcorn?

Who?
Who are some of the people that are famous in the history of popcorn?
Who is Orville Redenbacher and how did he get that way?
Who invented Cracker Jack?
Who invented the various types of popcorn poppers?

How?
How should popcorn be popped?
How did popcorn save movie theaters from bankruptcy?
How is popcorn used in some recipes?
How effective is popcorn as a health food?
How can I store popcorn?
How effective is popcorn as a diet food?

As you can see, I created many more topics than I could possibly handle in one article and I also had to accomplish considerable research to answer all these questions. But that's what your goal is when you're brainstorming. Write everything down, no matter how inappropriate it may seem. Do not critically judge your ideas at this point. Judgement day comes later when you research and outline your article.

Once you have accumulated a large number of questions, copy each question on a separate index card. You'll need these individual cards later when you research and record your answers to these questions on the cards.

This technique works for both fiction and nonfiction. For fiction the "who" is your character and you will be searching for ideas of why a character would do a particular thing, "how" he or she did it, "why" your character did it, and "where" and "when" he or she did something.

Ask specific questions

Asking yourself specific questions is another excellent way to brainstorm, because questions are the creative acts of the mind. Read through the questions listed below slowly and see which can be applied to your topics, your events.

For nonfiction and fiction, ask yourself, can I:

- Use a different shape, a different form? Use a different setting for my story?
- Make it faster, less expensive, smaller, lighter? Change the sequence of events in my story?
- Add new features to make it more versatile? Add more complications in my novel to enhance conflict?
- Combine it with something else? Combine two characters to make a new character? Break one character up into two characters?
- Reverse it, change the sequence? Change the time period of the story?
- Find new applications for it? Develop new conflicts for my main character?

- Use different components to obtain new proper-
  ties? Add new characters to enhance conflict
  and suspense?
- Adapt ideas from a related product, process?
  Adapt ideas from other stories?
- Split it up into smaller parts? Break the story up
  into smaller or larger scenes or sequels?
- Use a different process? Use a different view-
  point character?
- Merge old ideas? Merge small scenes or sequels
  to create bigger and more important scenes or
  sequels?

Brainstorming is not a 15-minute exercise. It may take
an hour or eight hours, perhaps much longer if you have
a complex subject to handle. But this is *prime time*. This
session gives you much of the basis, the framework for
your book, your article, your story, the topics or events, the
unique ideas, the thoughts you are going to cover.

This is the truly creative part of your writing. It is the
task that can make your book, your article, your novel an
outstanding one.

Go through your old and new idea cards a few more
times. More and more ideas will occur. Write them down,
uncritically, and you'll be amazed at how quickly the stack
of cards has grown into a full deck. When you feel your
creative juices have finally run their course, set all of your
notes aside and engage in some other activity for a few
hours.

Take a walk, ride your bike, shoot some baskets, hit a
few golf balls, do something physical to rest your mind
and let your subconscious go to work. If you can spare the
time, sleep on it.

Come back later and try to continue where you left off.
It's likely that your subconscious mind worked when you
were relaxing and created some new ideas. If so, continue
your brainstorming session. If it doesn't work, you've
probably done enough, so quit and go on to the next step of
your writing.

In the next chapter you're going to learn how to make effective use out of the most important technological advance made for writers since the printing press: the Personal Computer.

Exercises

1. Brainstorm a subject for an article or a book and come up with at least 20 pertinent facts, questions and ideas.
2. Brainstorm an idea for a short story or a novel and create at least 20 events, ideas and plot complications.

Chapter 6

The PC:
A Writer's Most
Valuable Tool

"Man is a tool-using animal."
Thomas Carlyle

Whether you opt to write longhand, type, dictate, or compose your article using a personal computer is your decision. If you have a choice, a personal computer (PC), the greatest writer's aid of modern times, is by far the best option. When I use the term "personal computer," I mean to encompass *all* personal computers, including IBM and its clones, the Macintosh, etc.

No tool in recent history has had a more positive and revolutionary impact on the art and science of writing and has taken so much of the drudgery out of writing, as the PC.

The most widely used application of the PC (an estimated 75 percent) is as a word processor (WP). Time and again researchers have demonstrated that writing with a word processor improves the quality of writing for anyone. And more and more publishers are requiring that books, articles and short stories be submitted on computer diskettes.

A WP automates much of the mechanics of your writing, making it easier to do. Unlike using a typewriter, you don't have to worry about hitting the carriage return at the end of a line, a carriage return is generated automatically. No matter how fast or how slow you type, a WP can keep pace with you. Text is automatically scrolled so you can continue typing and watch the material you input appear on the screen instantly.

If you're an inept typist, you can, and should, forget all about errors when you're inputting your first drafts of creative prose. You can go back later and easily edit all your mistakes, without losing any of your input, and without having to retype the entire document as you had to do in the olden days of the typewriter.

More positive about writing

Researchers have demonstrated that people who once dreaded writing have become much more positive about the craft once they have learned to write with a word processor. Another important fact favoring the use of the word processor is that researchers have discovered that our short-term memory lasts only about five seconds. A word processor can record your ideas much faster than you can input them, so your own typing speed, and not the computer's, are the limit in capturing your ideas.

Many auxiliary programs are available to help you create near-perfect text. Spelling programs, thesauruses, word counters, and programs to check sentence length are available.

Word processors are the wave of the future. The days of the handwritten or typewritten draft are nearly gone. Soon the only typewriters you'll be able to find will be in closets and museums. Before long we'll deliver much of our manuscripts as soft copy via modems, over telephone lines, to our publishers.

Computer knowledge not needed

You don't have to understand how computers function to use a word processor, any more than you need to know the electronic theory of television to operate a TV set. You need to learn only a few simple commands. When you first start using a WP and learning its commands, you're exercising the rational/logical part of your brain. And when you use the rational/logical part, it tends to inhibit the creative/intuitive part. So, for a short time using a word processor may handicap your writing, just as a typewriter did when you first started to use it.

However, once you've learned the basic commands, you'll discover that operating a word processor is largely transparent. That means you can type and perform all of the necessary commands and not be conscious of doing them, just as you do when you walk, drive an automobile, or use a typewriter. This is the point of reward. This is when operating a WP becomes automatic and your creative/intuitive function begins to assert itself. Once you reach this stage, you are truly accomplishing creative writing. This is a magic time, a time when writing becomes an exciting adventure, a pleasure.

When you begin to feel comfortable using a WP, it's very easy to stop and make corrections when you're inputting. However, when writing your creative drafts, resist this impulse. All you should do in the early stages of writing is get your ideas, your sentences, your thoughts down and stored in a magnetic media that you can access later. This important creative period should not be restricted by grammar, spelling, or other vital matters of form that can be attended to later during rewrites.

Word processor capabilities

When you choose a WP program, make sure it has the following capabilities as a minimum:

Help Menu. Should be accessible at all times, regardless of the writing mode you're in. Help Menus should be "context sensitive" and summarize the major functions of all the key commands.

Insert Mode. The Insert Mode lets you add information in any section of a manuscript. The text that follows the insert moves over to make room for the new text. This lets you start working with any module you choose and add any amount of information, in any part of your manuscript, and repeatedly switch back and forth between modules, and still keep everything in order.

Delete. You should be able to delete a letter, a word, to the end of a line, and large, selected blocks of text.

Oops! Command. Your WP should be able to temporarily store your latest delete operation in case you make a mistake (Oops!) and want the original version back.

Block Move. Needed to move large sections of your manuscript from one location to another. This is often referred to as "electronic cut-and-paste."

Search. This automatically searches for, then positions your cursor on the desired part of your writing for revision, review, and correction. You should be able to search "globally," that is, search forwards or backwards for a specific word or phrase throughout the entire document.

Search and Replace. Corrects spelling errors or changes words selectively or automatically in your text.

Copy. The copy function lets you copy words, phrases, or large parts of your manuscript, then move and insert them in other parts of your manuscript.

Underline. To highlight words, phrases, and titles.

Boldface. For your headings, subheadings.

Tab Set. To set indents, table formats, etc.

Centering. For figure titles, table titles, etc.

Full Justify. To provide neat-looking copy blocks, aligned with the left and right margins on your printouts.

Line Length. To set the line length to meet the special requirements of various manuscript formats.

Graphics. Some of the more advanced word processors can draw simple graphics (block diagrams, flow charts, tables, etc.) on the screen and print the text out on a dot matrix or laser printer, an extremely useful capability.

Print. To output your text on paper. Usually a dot matrix printer operating in a NLQ (Near Letter Quality) mode provides an acceptable hard copy. For complex graphics or very high-quality text, or unique fonts, a laser or ink-jet printer is desirable.

Print Spooling. The ability to print one document at the same time you're working on a different document.

Cancel/Pause Print. You should be able to cancel a printout in progress if you change your mind, or if you want to pause so you can input information manually.

Diskette Storage. In the future, publishers may require you to submit manuscripts on a diskette, in addition to a printed copy, to save the added burden of manually inputting your prose into the computer.

It would be a plus if your program had these capabilities as well:

Speller. A spelling program is excellent for correcting your misspelled words. The speller should also catch double words and be able to add words to a special dictionary to store some of the special words, names, or jargon that you use in your manuscripts. Your speller should be able to correct words "in context," that is, display them in your text so you can verify their usage.

Thesaurus. Helps locate synonyms.

Double-column Printing. The ability to print out double column is desirable for newsletters, manuals, etc.

Macros. Macros provide useful shortcuts, such as assigning a special key to type in complicated words, or to automatically set up a format, etc. A macro is a simple computer command, a mini-program that combines and reduces a WP command requiring a number of programmed strokes to one- or two-key strokes.

Word Count. Some qpellers can count the number of words in your text. This eliminates considerable tedium.

Contents/Index Generation. More and more word processors are incorporating the ability to automatically generate lists for contents, illustrations and tables pages, and for compiling an index.

Diskette storage capability

One "byte" represents a single character—it may be a letter, a symbol, or a space. An average word length is six characters, so even a low capacity, 300K (300,000) byte diskette can hold about 50,000 words.

Other high-density diskettes can hold more than one million bytes. An average double-spaced page contains approximately 250 words, so even a low-capacity diskette can hold almost 100 pages of writing. You'll never have to worry about running out of storage space on a new diskette, unless you're writing a huge book. However, graphics require considerable more space than text, typically about 10K or more for even simple graphics.

Graphics: Pictures save words

Most writers are "word oriented." By that I mean that they use only words to discuss or illuminate topics that could be better explained with a proper combination of words and graphics. Illustrations not only help in understanding difficult concepts, they also break up the forbidding task of facing a solid page of closely spaced words. Graphics provide better understanding as well as much-needed "eye relief."

Graphics or illustrations have, until now, been difficult for most writers to create. As graphic programs become easier and more convenient to use, and more versatile in their application, graphics are serving an increasingly important role in writing.

Exercises

1. List ten capabilities that a PC word processor provides over earlier writing methods.
2. What are the advantages of using graphics in writing?

Chapter 7

Research: How to Find Information Fast

"The man is most original who can adopt from the greatest number of sources."
Thomas Carlyle

When a college freshman returned a volume of Shakespeare to the library, he was asked what he thought of the bard's writing.

"I don't see why people make such a fuss over his work. All he does is bring together a bunch of old, well-known quotations."

Your task in conducting research is to profit from all those "old, well-known quotations" and to adapt, learn from, and expand on the information that your predecessors have documented.

Whether you write fiction or nonfiction, it's unlikely that you'll be able to create an entire article, a short story, a nonfiction book, or a novel completely by brainstorming. You'll probably have to conduct some research to verify facts for an article, research statistics for a book, check the style of clothing and the mode of living for a short story, or determine which world events shaped and influenced events in your novel. To find this information, you're going to have to research to locate the material you require to add authenticity and accuracy to your writing. And if your writing is good enough, you can create a work that future freshmen can quote from.

Your source

> *"If a man will begin with certainties, he shall end in doubts; but if he will be content to begin with doubts, he shall end in certainties."*
> Francis Bacon

Six excellent sources, all of which will be covered in this chapter, for finding information are:

1. Your personal library
2. Your local free library
3. New and used bookstores
4. The telephone
5. Online databases
6. The mail box

To begin your search, you need to know:

- What precisely are you looking for?
- When did it happen?
- To what depth must you research?

What precisely are you looking for?

This may seem obvious. But you must define *precisely* what you're looking for, or you will waste considerable time and effort. For example, assume research is needed to find:

- The number of farmers in the United States
- The Mark Fein murder case
- How a VCR operates
- The mode of women's dress in England

When did it happen?

To narrow down and speed up your research, you must establish a time frame in which it occurred. Did it happen yesterday, or last year, or the Spring of 1930, or about 1458? Is your information available in encyclopedias, or books, or old newspapers, or recent periodicals? Use the "when" to narrow the scope of the topics listed above:

- Number of farmers in the United States in 1942
- The Mark Fein murder case in 1963
- How the latest VCRs operate
- Mode of women's dress in England in 1720

To what depth must you research?

Do you need a few obscure facts, or do you need to conduct an in-depth search? Must you consult many references, or do you just need to check and verify a few facts? Further narrowing the depth of the above topics helps identify potential research sources:

- Number of farmers in the U.S. in 1941—Located in the *Statistical Abstract of the United States.*
- The Mark Fein Murder in 1963—To write an in-depth article on this case, check the crime book section of your local library, and the newspaper files for around that period. Also check *Readers' Guide to Periodical Literature* to see if some periodicals have covered the murder. For a specific reference, check the 20-volume set, *Crimes and Punishment* (BPC Publishing Limited) 1974, volume 12, pp 74-82.
- How the latest VCRs operate—For an article, first check the latest science encyclopedias for an overall picture and understanding of VCRs. Then check the engineering section of the library for technical books on VCRs. If you can't locate the book you want there, check a book such as *Scientific, Medical, & Technical Books*

that gives an authoritative list of the most important scientific and technical books in print. Finally, check the indexes that deal with technical matters, such as *Applied Science and Technology Index* to find articles in technical periodicals that discuss the latest VCRs from various manufacturers.

• Mode of women's dress in England in 1720— Check the Dewey Decimal 391 section of your local library. They generally have books with illustrations and photos of the clothes people wore at specific times in history. A specific reference is *What People Wore* by Douglas Gorsline (Bonanza Books), which gives a visual survey of dress that covers more than 5,000 years of history.

This chapter will cover the varied library resources and the wide variety of other resources available via your telephone, your mailbox and the rapidly emerging online databases. Also covered are the most efficient methods of locating the information you need in these resources.

Two kinds of knowledge

"Knowledge is of two kinds. We know a subject ourselves, or we know where we can find information upon it."
Samuel Johnson

To paraphrase Samuel Johnson a bit, the next best thing to knowledge is knowing where to acquire knowledge. Some of the best repositories of knowledge are public, private and university libraries. A phenomenal amount of information is available in libraries, but sometimes the sheer magnitude makes it very difficult to locate exactly what you're looking for in these mountains of knowledge. This chapter will show you what to look for, and how to find it in the most expeditious manner.

Professional researchers say it's better to know where to find a fact than it is to find the fact. In this book the emphasis is on knowing *where to find a fact.*

What researchers need to know

When you're about to research a subject you're going to write about and need to know what has been published in a similar vein, when you want to learn how people lived and loved, what they ate, how much a laborer earned for a day's work, and how many pounds of popcorn movie theaters sell in a year, you need to research the literature. Knowing where to look, how to look, and what to look for, can save you much valuable time.

Skilled librarians and abstracters spend hundreds of thousands of hours each year categorizing, cataloging, indexing, referencing, and abstracting the thousands of periodicals and books that are published. This chapter provides some shortcuts in locating the specific answers you need in the abundance of books and periodicals.

Books are the most important reference for research, but they are often out-of-date. Periodicals contain the most up-to-date information, but they generally do not cover subjects in adequate depth. So you need to learn how to search both sources to find the information you require to substantiate your writing.

Why conduct a search?

"The struggling for knowledge has a pleasure in it like that of wrestling with a fine woman."
George Savile, Lord Halifax

Reasons for researching the published literature are many and varied:

1. When you review printed works, you're often learning from the most skilled people in the field.
2. Often you'll get new ideas, new slants on your material when you review other writers' works.

Your creativity will be stimulated when you read what someone else wrote about a similar subject.

3. Since you have no personal knowledge, nor any memory of certain facts or customs, you need to review what historians and novelists have written about those topics.

4. If you need certain facts, you can't guess. You have to consult a reliable, factual document that has been prepared for that precise purpose.

A tremendous amount of information is available in those mountains of literature. And it's free. All it takes is a little time and effort, and some help in finding the proper direction for searching.

How to get started

"A great library contains the diary of the human race. The great consulting room of a well man is a library."
G. Dawson

First check the books you have at home. You should have at least one good dictionary, possibly a set of encyclopedias and an atlas, plus some reference books. If nothing else, checking these basic sources will help narrow down what you're looking for so you can locate precisely what you need from other sources. Articles in an encyclopedia usually have a bibliography listing references for more indepth searches.

Your next step should be toward that fount of knowledge, the library: a university, college, or good-sized public library. If you have trouble locating the right library, check one of these directories:

American Library Directory (ALD), R.R. Bowker Co. (2 volumes) (1923—). Lists more than 35,000 U.S. and Canadian libraries of all kinds: public, academic, company and associations. They're listed alphabetically by state and province and summarize each library's holdings. Since the directory has no subject index, use it to obtain information on a library whose name you already know, or libraries located in a specific city.

Directory of Special Libraries and Information Centers, 5 vols. Gale Research Co. (1963—). Issued every two years with supplements. Lists special collections and departments of libraries rather than libraries as a whole. The lists are arranged alphabetically by library regardless of its geographic location. A subject index is included.

Directory of Historical Societies and Agencies in the United States and Canada. American Association for State and Local History. (1956—). Issued every three years. Lists historical and genealogical societies in the U.S. and Canada. Arranged geographically.

Writers' Resource Guide, edited by Bernadine Clark. Writers' Digest Books. An excellent reference that is updated about every three years. Lists about 1,600 foundations, associations and companies. with information on the specific services they provide. Arranged in 30 subject chapters and indexed by subject and organization name.

The library you select may not have available all the material you're seeking, but they generally have most of the basic reference books, abstracts, and indexes you'll need. If they don't have a specific book, periodical, or document on hand, they can probably order it for you on an inter-library loan.

In your local library, begin by checking the card catalog that indexes all of its holdings. Many of the more modern libraries are converting to a computerized system where you can access all the libraries holdings from a computer terminal. No matter which system you use, the basics of finding information are still the same, so let's start with an old-fashioned manual card catalog.

Using the card catalog

In a card catalog, you can search for your topic by Subject, Author, or Title. (See an example of an Author card in Figure 19.) When you locate something of interest, be sure to write down the *full call number*, the *title*, and the *author* of the book or periodical on your index card notes. This not only helps you locate the specific book on the shelves, it also gives you a general location to browse through on the nearby shelves for related books on the same subject of interest. And if the book is checked out, the librarian will need this information to reserve it for you.

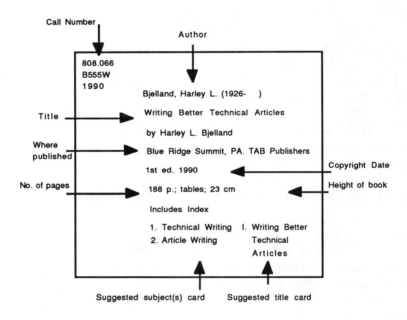

Figure 19. Author Library Card

Electronic card catalogs

Many libraries have converted their more recent and new acquisitions to computerized card catalogs and are gradually adding their older acquisitions to their computer data base.

Computerization of the library's holdings offers many additional features not possible with a manual card system. You can usually find what you're looking for in a much shorter time. You can search by author, title, subject, and call number and combinations of these. You can also search when you know only part of a title, name, subject or call number. And you can search with only a truncated name such as using "organiz" if you're not sure your reference is listed under "organizing," "organization," or "organized."

The computerized search will provide you with a list of books, plus additional bibliographic information about the specific book you search for. In addition, the computerized system can tell you if the book is checked out, and if it is, when it is due back, excellent features also not practical in a manual system. If you have a long list of references, ask your librarian to give you a printout so you won't have to write them all down.

General references

For a general, broad picture of a subject or a topic to help orient yourself at the start of a literature search, general reference books are often a great help. Usually these books do not have up-to-date information, but they do provide a good background to start with. They also have authoritative lists of additional references to check.

General reference books are listed in Appendix A of this book. The title is listed first, followed by the author (if one is listed), then the publisher. A date such as (1941—) means they first started publishing in 1941 and still are.

Books on reference sources

An excellent place to begin if you have no idea where to start looking are these general reference books.

A World Bibliography of Bibliographies—Besterman (1965-66). 5 vol. Includes 117,000 items, grouped under 16,000 headings and subheadings. A classified bibliography of separately published bibliographies of books, manuscripts, and patent abridgements. International in scope.

American Reference Books Annual—Littleton, CO: Libraries Unlimited (1970—). Annual. Each issue covers the reference output (including reprints) of the previous years. Offers descriptive and evaluative notes with references to selected reviews. Classed arrangement; author-subject-title index.

Bibliographic Index—A cumulative bibliography of bibliographies. Wilson (1938—). An alphabetical subject arrangement of separately published bibliographies, and of the bibliographies included in books and periodicals. About 2,600 periodicals are examined regularly.

Government Reference Books—Libraries Unlimited (1970—). Biennial. Annotated list of bibliographies, directories, dictionaries, statistical works, handbooks, almanacs, and similar reference sources published by the U.S. Government. Classed arrangement with author-title-subject index. Includes Superintendent of Documents classification numbers.

Guide to Reference Books—Eugene P. Sheehy. Chicago; American Library Association (1986—). Subject, title, and author index of sources in all fields. Special section on pure and applied sciences. An excellent, comprehensive guide. **The best!**

New and used bookstores

If you can't locate the book or can't obtain it on an inter-library loan, check the new and used bookstores. For the latest book on your subject, your local bookstore either has it or can get it for you on short order. Used bookstores often have excellent selections of books and usually sell them for half the cover price. When you're finished with the book, you can sell it back to them for half of what you've paid for it or you may want to keep the book for your permanent collection.

How to locate experts

If you find yourself stumped in your library research and need to obtain information or assistance with your topics, there are a number of ways to locate experts. When you have the name of an expert, first check your phone book (or one for the city in which your expert lives—out-of-city phone books are usually available in the library).

Next, check a directory such as *Who's Who in America, American Men and Women of Science, Faculty Directory*, etc. These directories usually provide a mailing address and often a telephone number.

If you're beginning with a topic and don't have a title or a name, check the *Subject Guide to Books In Print*. This excellent reference lists in-print and forthcoming titles (except fiction) by one author and uses the Library of Congress subject headings. Then you can check a reference such as *Who's Who* to obtain the author's address and affiliation.

More sources

Most experts belong to one or more associations. *The Encyclopedia of Associations* published by Gale Research lists these associations. Write or phone the headquarters of the specific association to locate your expert.

For all-around coverage of topics, contact the National Referral Center of the Library of Congress, Washington, D.C. (202) 287-5000. Contact: Referral Services Section. The NRC refers people who have a question on any subject to organizations that can provide the answers.

NRC keeps an up-to-date database of more than 13,000 information resources. The inquiry is referred *free of charge* to the proper organization. The database may be searched online at the Library of Congress and also through the DOE/RECON network maintained by the Department of Energy.

If you need to contact a government agency, the best directory is the *U.S. Government Manual*. It details the organization, the major activities and the chief officers of the offices in all three branches of government. Contact the Superintendent of Documents, Government Printing Office, Washington, D.C. 20402. (202) 783-3238. Order by stock number 022-003-01082-3.

People to call

The telephone is an excellent research tool that gives you instantaneous answers. Among the resources you can utilize from your telephone are:

1. Your local library—ask for the reference desk. They'll gladly look up short facts for you and give you a quick answer.
2. Your local newspaper
3. Companies and services that are listed in the yellow pages
4. An expert on your subject

Regardless of who you call, observe a few important rules of etiquette. Following these will help ensure that your call will give you the information you seek.

But before you call, make some notes to yourself. You might even write out how you want to introduce yourself and also write down your first question exactly as you are going to ask it. In addition, make notes on other questions you want to ask, other information you are looking for to remind you as you are talking to your expert. Often when you talk without prepared notes, you are distracted and forget to ask some of the questions. Write down the expert's name, affiliation, and any pertinent facts you may have about him or her before you call. If in your conversation you're referred to another expert, make sure you get that new expert's full name, spelling, affiliation, and phone number.

The mailbox

Another excellent but often overlooked resource is the mail. For the price of a couple of stamps you can contact some of these sources:

1. The government
2. Trade and professional organizations
3. Experts on your topics

When you write to any of these experts, make your questions concise and specific. Number them. If your questions are short enough so that your expert can write the answers on the same page as your letter, leave a little room for that. Or if you have an extensive list of questions, use a second sheet, list all the questions there by number, and leave room for the answers. Most experts don't particularly like to take the time and effort required to write letters, but I have found them to be much more receptive to writing in their answers.

Make sure you enclose a stamped, self-addressed envelope for the reply. This can often make the difference between receiving and not receiving a reply.

How to take notes

"The secret of good writing is to say an old thing in a new way or to say a new thing in an old way."
Richard Harding Davis

Now that you know where to locate your information, you should cultivate an efficient and accurate note-taking procedure. When you read something you want to make a note of, read it over carefully, let it sink in your mind. Then paraphrase it, restate it in your own words *immediately*.

If you can paraphrase it, that means you understand it. Also note the source and the date of the original information you have just paraphrased in case you have to check back later to verify something.

When you take notes, it's a good practice to *always* paraphrase the information before you write it down so you can't be accused of plagiarism. Plagiarism comes from the Latin word for "kidnapping." It's all right to adapt material, but don't kidnap anyone's writing.

Don't tell yourself that you'll paraphrase it later. You probably won't remember if you paraphrased it originally, and the original you copied down may have sunk so deep into your subconscious that it will be difficult to paraphrase later. Or you may be in too much of a hurry to paraphrase it later. If you must copy verbatim, enclose the statement in quotes and note its origin.

The method I use in making notes follows: The best media I've found to record research notes on are index cards. They're stiff and easy to manipulate. One side is normally lined, the other blank. The cards are available in 3-by-5, 4-by-6, and 5-by-8 sizes. Choose a size that's big enough to contain your notes and stick with that size.

Here are some general guidelines to observe when you take notes:

1. Choose either the ruled or unruled side of the card for writing your notes. (I use the unruled side for my notes, because I occasionally incorporate a simple figure or illustration along with my notes. Also I think that lined writing material inhibits what and how much you can write.) Whichever you choose, be consistent. Write your notes on only one side of the card.

2. Put only *one* idea on a card. That way your cards will be easier to organize later into topics and subtopics using the Precedent Sort. An *idea* or *topic* may be defined as any small amount of information that will not have to be broken up so that the parts can be placed at separate points in your outline. At the top of each card (see Figure 20) put a title, or topic, or subject, or heading or whatever you'll need for reviewing them later. The heading on the card is called a "slug." The slug serves as a brief reminder, a summary of what's on the note card.

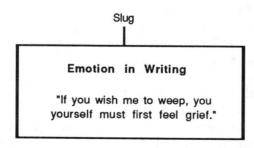

Figure 20. Index Card-Topic Title and Notes

3. Use the opposite side of the card (see Figure 21) to record bibliographic information. If the note is your own idea, record this fact on the bibliographic side. When you've accumulated a lot of notes, you may later have a difficult time remembering which ideas came from you, and which came from the references.

4. Take many more notes than you need. Some writers recommend taking twice as many notes as you need. Later you can prune them down and select the best of the best.

5. Don't use too much shorthand, you may forget what you meant by it. Record enough information to save yourself a trip back to the library.

6. Each card should have the following information as a minimum:

a. The book or periodical reference
b. The slug (Topic or subtopic title)
c. Your notes

Quote by Horace [65-8 B.C.]

Ars Poetica, 1.102

Figure 21. Index Card-Bibliographic Data

7. Read through your references carefully to make sure you understand them, then digest and paraphrase what you've read, put it in your own words. Write down key ideas, key words, key phrases.

8. Write carefully so you can read your own scribbling later. Few things are as annoying as to return home and be unable to decipher your scrambled handwriting.

When you conduct your research, you'll be taking three types of notes—quotations, paraphrasing and personal comments.

Copy verbatim only if your reference has said something unique. You'll find that about 90 percent of the time, you'll be paraphrasing the information. When the information is in your own words, it suits your purposes better than the quotation. And you can usually shorten it.

If you must use a quotation, such as quoting an expert or well-known person, put quotes around it, even if you paraphrase it later. Copy it exactly, including the punctuation, spelling, capitalization, and paragraphing. If you omit a part of the quotation that does not apply to your topic, indicate the omitted part with ellipses (...).

How to review books quickly

You're probably not going to have enough time to review in-depth all the books you'd like to research. Here are some shortcuts that will give you enough information for your material:

1. Skim the book. Get an overview of the whole before dealing with its parts. Check how it's organized. Read the chapter titles, the bold headings, study the illustrations. They'll give you a quick summary of the book's contents.

2. Read the title page, it may also have a subtitle. Note the author and his or her qualifications. Check the publication date to see how recently it's been published, or if it's only a reprint of an earlier edition. Note the publisher. The book is more likely to be an authoritative reference if the publisher specializes in that type of book.

3. Read the foreword, preface, introduction. They often give the purpose and intent of the book.

4. Review the Table of Contents; it outlines the book's contents.

5. Read the opening paragraphs of each chapter. Skim the contents of each chapter and make notes of any pertinent information.

6. For a more in-depth review of a book, read all of the topic sentences—that is, the first one or two

sentences of each paragraph. These often introduce and summarize the topics covered in the
paragraph in adequate detail to understand the
topic. If the topic is of specific interest, read the
entire paragraph.

7. Check the index for specific topics of interest
and see how many pages are devoted to these
topics. If you find some topics that pique you,
look them up, skim them and make any notes
that interest you.

8. Check the bibliography. It will reveal the
author's sources and whether he or she is
using up-to-date information.

Online systems: A revolution in research

An exciting revolution is underway that is radically
changing forever the look and operation of our public and
private libraries, the manner in which our newspapers
and books will exist, and the general way in which we
obtain information. Online systems databases, or electronic libraries, make searching for information feasible
and fast. Modern online system vendors allow you to tap
into gigantic databases, search millions of documents in
seconds, and view the result on your home or office personal computer. Suddenly any fact you need is as close as
your telephone.

What is a database?

A database is an organized collection of information
that a computer can search as a unit. A database can be a
telephone directory, it can be a series of books or periodicals, or full text versions of newspapers and articles, or a
computer readable version of an entire set of encyclopedias. Virtually any information that can be converted to
digital form can be made available for quick retrieval by a
computer. Many databases are collections of abstracts and
bibliographies from periodicals. Some databases are specific abstracts collected by specialty organizations. The

variety, depth, and diversity of available databases is mind-boggling. Databases are purchased by, or created by online vendors who sell access time to anyone wanting to search for information. Your computer, your modem, and your telephone give you the access to varied databases as illustrated in Figure 22.

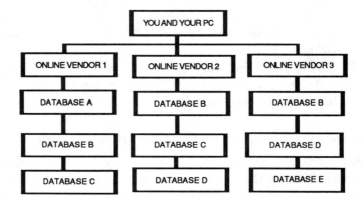

Figure 22. Database Varieties from Various Vendors

Why use databases?

Basic reasons for using a database when conducting research for your writing are:

- They help you quickly locate those few important bytes of data you need in that megabillion-mountain of information.
- You obtain instantaneous answers.
- Vendor's databases are much larger than public and private libraries.
- Information is up-to-date.
- Specialized databases exist for virtually every field of writing and for every profession.
- Information is available *when* you want it. You don't have to worry that someone has checked out the book or periodical you need to consult.

- The information is comprehensive. You can research to any depth you need.
- You can query from your home or office, from virtually any place that has a telephone. No longer do you have to waste time commuting, fighting city traffic and parking problems.

So, as you conduct research for your current and future writing, you may want to acquaint yourself with the application of online databases, the remotely located electronic libraries you can now access that are as close as your telephone.

Exercises

1. Choose a topic or subject and research it in a general encyclopedia. Note the references at the end of the encyclopedia article and review some of them to obtain more information. Take notes on what you have learned.
2. For this same topic, research it in more depth using a special reference. Take notes on what you have found out. Be sure you list the references you located them in.
3. Select a topic suitable for a short story or a novel, one that requires some library research for background material, customs of the times, etc. Locate some specific references that cover this material and take notes on it

Chapter 8

The Magic Three Elements of Writing

"Pythagoras called three the perfect number,
expressive of beginning, middle, and end."

Three has long been a magic number. Man is threefold (body, mind, and spirit), the enemies of man are threefold (the world, the flesh, and the devil), and the world is threefold (earth, sea, and air).

The Christian Trinity is threefold (Father, Son, and Holy Spirit), the Scandinavians' mythological "Mysterious Three" sit on three thrones in Asgard, and the Brahmans' God has three heads. The Fates are three, the Graces are three, and the Harpies are three.

Our lives are completed in three steps: Birth, Life and Death. Many fairy tales feature the magic number: "The Three Little Pigs," and "Goldilocks and the Three Bears." Most plays have three acts. The third illustration or example in a joke is usually the punch line.

Aristotle applied the magic number three to writing, "A whole is that which has a beginning, middle, and end." In this chapter you'll learn how to apply this universal, proven, centuries-old, magic number to your writing to create brilliant beginnings, magnificent middles, and exceptional endings.

Even in a sentence?

Most well-constructed sentences have three parts: a beginning, a middle, and an end. In the sentence you just finished reading, the beginning is "Most well-constructed sentences," the middle is the verb "have," and the end or conclusion is "three parts: a beginning, a middle, and an end."

Well-constructed sentences are composed in what is called a subject-verb-object (three-part) order; that is, in a things-doings-results order that is essentially the same as a beginning-middle-end order. The simple sentence, "Earl shot the tiger," puts everything in the proper order. First you "see" Earl, next the active verb "shot" gives you the action, then you see that the object he shot was a tiger and you can instantly compose the picture in your mind. If the sentence had been, "The tiger was shot by Earl," your mind would have been jerked out of gear. You would first see "The tiger," (what's it doing there?), then read, "was shot" (who shot it?) and finally "by Earl" (aha, but you told me a little too late. I'd rather "see" the one performing the action first).

Coleridge said, "Prose—words in their best order." The earlier sentence about Earl is in the "best order."

Not *all* sentences should follow this strict order. For variety, to help better explain certain concepts, and to avoid a monotonous, sing-song effect, use varied sentence constructions and different length sentences. (Note that the preceding sentence is in reverse order.) However, most sentences should use the recommended beginning-middle-end order. A few sentences (less than 25 percent according to some experts) should use a reverse order. But be extra careful when using a reverse order to make sure that your prose will not be misunderstood.

Parallelism

Another important grammatical device that improves and clarifies sentences, paragraphs, and even longer units of writing is *parallelism*. Parallelism is making sure that *parallel* ideas are stated in *parallel* structures.

To illustrate this important principle, consider this sentence:

> "Proper organization of your material helps you to plan what you're going to write, writing and revision of it."

This should be changed to a better and clearer construction by using parallelism:

> "Proper organization of your material helps you *to* plan what you're going to write, *to* write it, and *to* revise it."

Parallelism provides a strong sense of order to a reader. It unifies thoughts or ideas, it makes sentences easier to understand, and it clarifies relationships.

Paragraphs for nonfiction

Most nonfiction paragraphs should also be three parts. To better explain the functions of each component part of a nonfiction paragraph, we'll name them the Introduction, Body, and Conclusion, as illustrated by the paragraph pattern of Figure 23.

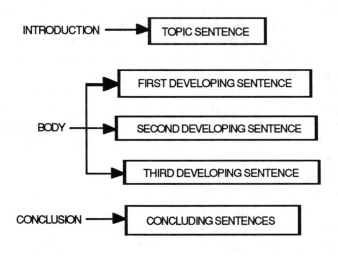

Figure 23. Paragraph Pattern

Here's an example of a paragraph pattern:

"However, computers will never replace the human brain. [Topic sentence, plus transition (however)]. In spite of the incredible advances in computer technology, these electronic marvels cannot create new ideas. (First developing sentence). Computers cannot devise a logical sentence, even with an enormous vocabulary stored in their memory. (Second developing sentence). Nor can computers be inspired, feel depressed or hungry, or become angry, emotions necessary to put emotion into writing. (Third developing sentence). So the computer will always remain our slave and we will always remain its master. (Concluding sentence)."

The **introduction** or *beginning* is usually a *topic sentence* and is often the first one or two sentences in a paragraph. The introduction also includes a transition from the previous paragraph (either direct or implied) and is often a general statement that summarizes and introduces the topic of the paragraph. The topic sentence usually introduces the whole, the developing sentences that follow in the body usually develop the part.

The **body**, or central portion of the paragraph expands on the topic. One or more *developing sentences* in the body then utilize data, illustrations, examples, or quotes to provide proof, explanation, or expansion. By the end of the body of a paragraph, a reader is ready for a *conclusion*.

The **conclusion** sums up what the topic covers and draws a conclusion from what has been discussed earlier in the paragraph. Sometimes a conclusion can easily be inferred from the body and does not need to be specifically stated. The conclusion is often the last one or two sentences in a paragraph.

Not every paragraph should follow this precise, somewhat restrictive pattern. For variety, to help better explain certain concepts, and to avoid predictable patterns, vary the construction of some of the paragraphs. Start some with a conclusion, then follow with the proofs for that conclusion. Place the developing sentences first, follow them with the topic sentence and the conclusion. But *do not* sacrifice clarity simply for the sake of variety. Above all, your paragraphs must be complete, logically organized, and easy-to-understand.

Fiction paragraphs

In fiction, paragraph divisions serve basically the same functions, except for dialogue. When dialogue is used in fiction, each new paragraph indicates a change in speaker.

Nonfiction modules

To continue up the ladder of a nonfiction book's hierarchy, the next rung, the module, is comprised of a number of consecutive paragraphs as shown in Figure 24.

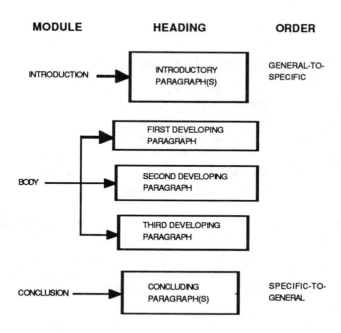

Figure 24. Module Pattern

Each module should contain a single idea, a single concept. For each module, the introductory one or two paragraphs become the beginning or introduction to that module. They introduce the whole before the developing paragraphs develop the part. They usually proceed from the general to the specific.

However, the specific-to-general may also be used for some paragraphs for clarity. An introductory paragraph(s) opens with a broad, general statement, then gradually narrows the focus down to the points to be covered in the module.

Each module should have:

- a heading
- a beginning paragraph(s)
- proof—One or more topics, related to each other, organized in a sequence—developing paragraphs
- an ending paragraph(s)

Body and conclusion for nonfiction

Several developing paragraphs are needed to form the body of the nonfiction module. The number of paragraphs to be used depends on how many topics you elect to include and how thorough you are going to cover them. These developing paragraphs are more technical, more detailed. In these paragraphs you provide more concrete and detailed discussions, descriptions, or quotes to support the introductory paragraphs. The sequential order in which this material is presented should be chosen from one of those listed in Chapter 2. As a general rule, proceed from the known-to-unknown. The supporting paragraphs should build up into more and more important points, with the most important point concluding the body of the module.

The reader will then be prepared to understand and accept the conclusion reached in the final paragraph of the module. The final paragraph concludes the module with a statement or a conclusion for the topic covered in the preceding paragraphs and that was introduced in the first paragraph. The concluding paragraph should have an inverse construction to that of the introductory paragraph(s). Starting with a general statement, sometimes by merely rewording the topic sentence, the concluding paragraph works its way toward a general, broad statement that can be concluded from the material that preceded it. This is the specific-to-general order.

Fiction modules

"A story is a chain of scenes and sequels."
Dwight V. Swain

The scene and sequel are two basic types of fiction modules. These modules are usually alternated to create a story:

The *scene* is a basic unit of a plot and can run anywhere in length from a paragraph to many pages. The length of a scene is a function of the intensity and duration of the conflict. The conflict can be verbal, physical, psychological, etc. The basic function of the scene is to arouse the reader's interest in the story. Scenes are fast-moving.

The *sequel* or aftermath is used between scenes to establish plausibility for your story and can range in length from a single sentence to a number of pages where the protagonist ponders his or her fate, makes a decision, and puts the decision into action. Sequels usually slow a story down. The sequel may also be viewed as a scene-to-scene transition

Scene module

The Scene module also follows the Magic Three formula with different designations:

- Goal (Introduction)
- Conflict (Body)
- Disaster (Conclusion)

In a scene module, the *goal* of the protagonist is the motivation for the Scene. The resultant *conflict* occupies much of the scene, building up into a situation that explodes, concluding with a *disaster* for the protagonist.

Unlike the positive conclusion typically used in a non-fiction module, the conclusion scene in a fiction module has to end up in the air, unsettled, in a disaster, so as to induce the reader to keep reading.

This disaster is a continuation or intensification of the conflict introduced earlier, or the introduction of a new conflict, or a new obstacle related to the existing conflict. The disaster is a "hook".

Sequel module

The sequel module also conforms to the Magic Three of writing and is composed of these three parts:

- Reaction (Introduction)
- Dilemma (Body)
- Decision (Conclusion)

The *reaction* is the emotion the protagonist feels, the way he or she reacts to the disaster of the previous scene. The reaction may be emotional, physical, psychological, etc.

For the second part of the sequel module, the protagonist faces a *dilemma* in trying to evaluate the effects of, and to decide what to do about the disaster.

In the *decision* part of the sequel module, the protagonist makes a decision and puts that decision into action. The next scene then follows this sequel.

General transitions

Transitions are the bridges that join all the writing elements together as listed in Table 2. This table also defines the content and functions of the various elements of a manuscript as defined in this book.

The manuscript consists of one or more chapters, tells the whole story, and is designated by a title (***The Write Stuff***).

ELEMENT	TRANSITIONS	CONTAINS
MANUSCRIPT	TITLE	ONE OR MORE CHAPTERS
CHAPTER-MAJOR IDEA	TITLE AND/OR NUMBER	ONE OR MORE MODULES
MODULE-MULTIPLE IDEAS	HEADING OR PHYSICAL SPACE ON PAGE	ONE OR MORE PARAGRAPHS
PARAGRAPH MINOR IDEA	INDENTATION AND WHITE SPACE	ONE OR MORE SENTENCES
SENTENCE-MULTIPLE THOUGHTS	PERIOD, QUESTION MARK, EXCLAMATION MARK	ONE OR MORE CLAUSES
CLAUSE-MAJOR THOUGHT	COMMA, SEMICOLON, COLON	SUBJECT PLUS VERB-ONE OR MORE PHRASES
PHRASE - MINOR THOUGHT	TWO OR MORE WORDS	HEAD WORD AND ONE OR MORE SUBSIDIARY WORDS
WORD-SMALLEST ELEMENT OF COMMUNICATION	SINGLE SPACE OR DASH	WORD

Table 2. Transitions

The next level down, the chapter, contains a major idea (The Magic Three) and is comprised of one or more modules. For nonfiction, the transition from chapter-to-chapter is a chapter number and/or a chapter title. For fiction, the chapter-to-chapter transition is simply a new page, a new chapter number, and a continuation of the plot.

The module contains multiple ideas and is comprised of one or more paragraphs. The transition from module-to-module for nonfiction is usually a bold or underlined heading. For fiction, the module-to-module transitions are usually a physical spacing (double space) between the ending and beginning paragraphs and a continuation of the plot.

The paragraph contains a minor idea and is composed of one or more sentences. The transition from paragraph to paragraph is indicated by a simple indentation and surrounding white space for both fiction and nonfiction and a continuation of related topics or events. For dialogue in fiction, paragraph-to-paragraph transitions indicate a change in speaker .

The next level down, the sentence has one or more clauses and contains a multiple thought. Sentence-to-sentence transitions are indicated by specific punctuation marks such as a period, question mark, and exclamation mark and a one- or two-space separation before the beginning of the next sentence.

The clause contains a major thought and has a subject and a verb. Clause-to-clause transitions are also designated by specific punctuation: comma, semicolon, and colon. The phrase is a minor thought element and is made up of a head word, plus one or more subsidiary words. The transition from phrase-to-phrase is one or more words. The word contains a minor thought and is the smallest element of communication. The word-to-word transition is a single space.

Word and topic transitions

In addition to the transitions indicated in Table 2, other types of transitions are needed to connect the various writing elements. A topic transition should exist between all the major elements. The actual transitions may be implied by a continuation of the plot (for fiction) or continuation of the topic (for nonfiction).

For smaller transitions (paragraph-to-paragraph, for example), transitions may be direct (repetition of words or use of synonyms) or implied (continuation of the plot or further discussion of the topic.)

Transitions are a vital part of **all** writing. They should be so smooth and so logical as to be completely transparent. The reader should not be able to detect any jump in continuity.

Nonfiction chapter

Now we're nearing the top rungs of the ladder of composition: the Chapter. The basic pattern of a chapter is illustrated in Figure 25. The Chapter Title summarizes the contents of the chapter.

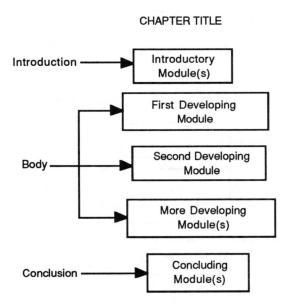

Figure 25. Nonfiction Chapter Pattern

The first or introductory module of each chapter should summarize the topics to be covered in that chapter. Each topic should first be introduced by its topic name, then a short summary of what is to be covered about each topic should follow. By the end of the first module of each chapter, the reader has been prepared for the topics to be covered next in the *body of the chapter*.

The body of each chapter is comprised of a number of developing modules that, by adding more and more illustrations, examples, anecdotes, data, quotes, etc. (a wider variety of expansion methods can be used here) further expand the topic of the chapter.

Finally the conclusion module of the chapter provides a conclusion, a statement, and a climax. The end of a chapter is often a convenient place to set the book aside. To prevent this, a "hook" should be included as the last few sentences of each chapter to hook or entice the reader into continuing reading.

Fiction chapter

For fiction, a similar pattern is used as illustrated in Figure 26.

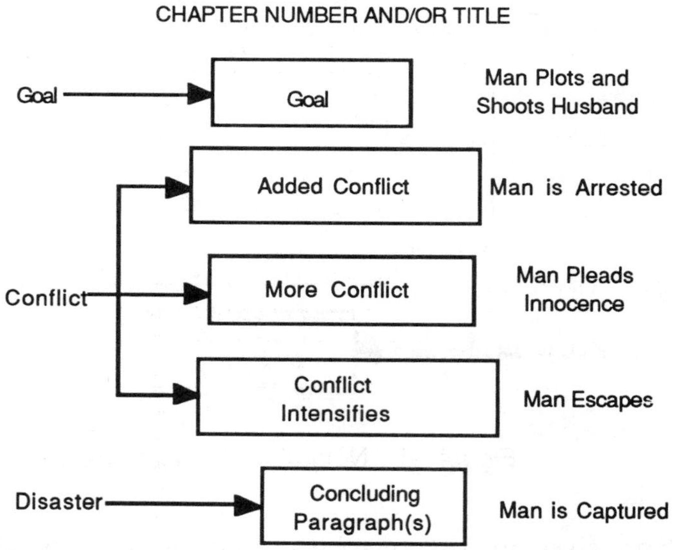

CHAPTER NUMBER AND/OR TITLE

Goal ──────▶	Goal	Man Plots and Shoots Husband
	Added Conflict	Man is Arrested
Conflict ─┬─▶	More Conflict	Man Pleads Innocence
	Conflict Intensifies	Man Escapes
Disaster ──────▶	Concluding Paragraph(s)	Man is Captured

Figure 26. Fiction Scene Pattern

The book

The largest division, the *book*, should also follow the magic three parts. Notice that Chapter 1 in this book is an introduction, and includes a preamble to the general topics, plus a summary of all the chapters in the entire book to prepare the reader for what is to follow.

Chapters 2 through 12 form the body of this book and are my proofs, my examples, my illustrations, my anecdotes, my quotes, and my data that collectively should combine to prove the topic of the book stated in its title, *The Write Stuff*. The final chapter, Chapter 13, "Good Writing Techniques," is a conclusion, an end, a summary, and brings together much of what was covered in the earlier chapters, and draws some conclusions.

In a novel, a similar situation exists. In the first chapter, your protagonist has an initial goal. Throughout the other chapters the protagonist alternately solves and is then confronted with more and more complications, more and more disasters, until he or she faces the final disaster and either overcomes the final challenge, or is consumed by it.

Limited attention span

When you get ready to write, remember that your reader doesn't have much time. Your reader is impatient, anxious for you to get to the point. Reading your prose should require a minimum of effort on your reader's part.

For example, when you give a speech, the first one or two minutes are all important, because that will probably be the only time that everyone will be listening. The attention span of audiences is woefully short.

Similarly, when you write your first few paragraphs of each chapter and of each module, they are very important because they may be the *only* part of your writing that will be read. Readers' attention spans are also woefully short.

Coming up...

Chapter 9 and Chapter 11 explain the principles of top-down planning and bottom-up writing a manuscript. Then, to follow the sage advice of Samuel Johnson, "Example is always more efficacious than precept," Chapter 10 and Chapter 12 illustrate the principles taught throughout the book by examples showing how to create an article, and a short story. The article can be considered as one chapter of a nonfiction book. The short story can be considered the equivalent of one chapter of a novel. So the same procedures can be used repeatedly to build an article or a short story up into a complete book. Because of space limitations, only selected portions of the examples will be used in this book.

In case you missed it (and I hope that you did), the previous paragraph is a hook to induce you to read on. Sorry I had to remove the transparency and point out the hook because it takes some of the effectiveness out of it if readers know what you're doing to them.

So, read on and make some new discoveries.

Exercises

1. List at six things that are also comprise of three parts, such as the wedding vows: Love, Honor, and Obey.
2. Write a paragraph that has a definable Introduction, Body, and a Conclusion.

Chapter 9

The Universal
Top-down
Design Subroutine

---

*"Write the way an architect builds, who first
drafts his plan and designs every detail."*
Arthur Schopenhauer

Although a variety of special formats are required for
different types of fiction and non-fiction manuscripts, the
basic procedures for planning and writing them are very
similar. This chapter develops the first of two universal
procedures: the procedure for top-down *designing*
(planning) a manuscript. Chapter 11 develops the second,
the procedure for bottom-up *writing* of a manuscript.

The following manuscript formats will be covered:

- Short stories
- Non-fiction articles

In this chapter, and in the chapters that follow, these
universal procedures will be developed and applied to
illustrate in detail how to top-down design and bottom-up
write both the short story (or one chapter of a novel) and
the article (or one chapter of a nonfiction book or of a
report).

Universal procedures

In addition to adapting the Precedent Sort from computer programming principles, I also investigated the applicability of two other concepts of computer technology for use in fiction and nonfiction writing. After years of research and experimentation, I developed universal procedures that are basically the same for all writing formats and that can be used for any type of manuscript longer than a letter or memo.

I call these universal procedures "subroutines" because they function much like the subroutines used in computer programming. A *computer subroutine* is a fixed sequence of commands used repeatedly in a computer program. A *writing subroutine* is a procedure that is followed repeatedly in designing and writing a manuscript.

Writing subroutines

The two basic writing subroutines that will be covered are:

1. Top-down design (planning) of a manuscript
2. Bottom-up writing of the designed manuscript

Instead of "planning," I prefer to use "design" for the first of the subroutines because when you are planning a manuscript, you are actually designing it.

All manuscripts should be *designed* from the top-down. You begin at the very top with a title, or an idea, or a purpose, or a theme. Then you top-down design lower and lower level details (chapters, modules, etc.) until you reach the lowest level of detail (module or submodule).

The second major subroutine, *writing*, uses the same principles utilized in writing a computer program. A computer program is written from the bottom-up, starting with basic computer commands, building up into more and more detail, adding more and more subroutines until the program is completed. Similarly, after a manuscript is designed from the top-down, it is also written from the bottom-up, starting with words, building up into phrases, clauses, sentences, etc., until the entire manuscript is completed according to the top-down design plan.

Because of the detailed outline created by applying these two basic and universal subroutines, modular writing permits designing and writing *any* section of a manuscript, *in any order* that is optimum for you, the designer, the writer, the creator of the manuscript. No longer do you have to proceed straight from the beginning to the end of your story, your novel, your article, your report.

You can begin where your inspiration leads you, then top-down design and bottom-up write your modules for your masterpiece in any order you choose. You can top-down design and bottom-up write one module at a time if that works best for you. Or you can top-down design a number of modules, then bottom-up write a single module at a time if that choice is optimum. Modular writing gives you the complete freedom and the total flexibility to tailor your writing and design processes in any order that is best for you and for your topic, your plot.

In the remainder of this chapter I'll develop the top-down design subroutine in detail. In the next chapter I'll show how to use the top-down design subroutine to design an original short story and an original article. Chapter 11 will develop the *bottom-up writing subroutine* in detail. Chapter 12 will show how to apply the bottom-up writing subroutine to write an original short story and an article.

Order: A necessity

A writer who begins by writing a paragraph or module of a manuscript before an overall *plan* or *outline* has been created has entered a circuitous maze. Without direction, a writer cannot create a logical progression of related topics, compose a coherent plot, create a sequence of scenes and sequels, nor write a complete manuscript that is readable, easily understood, and entertaining. Order is necessary to provide this direction.

In the process of top-down design you establish order by progressing from an abstract idea (title of book) to lesser abstract ideas (titles of chapters) to more concrete ideas, breaking your writing up into modules.

It's very difficult for a person with an active mind, such as a writer has, to channel his or her total energies on one narrow aspect of a topic, to the exclusion of all other topics. Most likely you'll be designing one module and suddenly have an inspiration that fits in a different module. That's where your detailed outline comes in handy. When you get your inspiration, grab hold of it. Make a note of it, then continue designing where you left off. Later, when you review the module for which you had your sudden inspiration, you can integrate your new idea into the appropriate place in your outline.

Kinship: Writing and computer programming

You may not realize it, but every time you press a key on your word processor, you activate a number of subroutines that programmers have created. A subroutine is a basic computer process that is stored in your computer and used repeatedly, such as the subroutine your computer uses to delete a specific letter on your screen. Each time you press the delete key, the same subroutine is activated and always performs the *same* function in the *same* way.

The more computer programming and writing I accomplished, the more I detected a close relationship between computer programming and writing, two seemingly opposite disciplines. Writing does indeed bear a strong similarity to computer technology because when you write a manuscript you create and repeatedly activate a number of subroutines: a design-a-module subroutine, a write-a-paragraph subroutine, a write-a-module subroutine, etc. So I began to explore the interrelationships between the two professions.

Universal subroutine for top-down design

One significant advantage of this top-down or "hierarchal" design approach is that you don't have to think about the little details (the words and the paragraphs) at the same time you're trying to decide the major issues (creating the chapters, the modules). Top-down design lets you divide the subject of your manuscript into separate entities of similar size and of similar scope.

Each entity is self-sufficient and can then be dealt with, one at a time. Once properly defined, each entity can be further broken down. Top-down design does this by breaking the Herculean task of writing an entire manuscript down into individual, easy-to-accomplish steps.

Figure 27 diagrams the universal, step-by-step subroutine for top-down designing any component part of any manuscript. A "component" is a general term that is defined as a specific portion of a manuscript...a chapter, a module, or a submodule (series of paragraphs). This universal subroutine can be used repeatedly to design any of these basic components.

Select title/theme/purpose

If you are just beginning to design your manuscript, your first component will be your title, your theme, or your purpose, or some combination of these that you will use to form and guide the detailed design of your individual components. You must design the "whole" before you design the "parts."

Selecting a title/theme/purpose may be the easiest or the most difficult step. The title you select may be only a tentative or working title. However, your theme and/or purpose must be clearly defined before you begin to outline, because this defines your slant, the manner in which you view the material, the type of research to be done, and the message or information you wish to convey. Your goal may be simply to entertain, or you may wish to deliver a message, or you may want to inform readers about something. This basic decision establishes the direction for your work.

If you already have a title/theme/purpose, you should write your title/theme/purpose down to demonstrate to yourself that you have clearly and precisely defined what you are going to write about. If you can't describe your title/purpose/theme in a few clear, succinct statements, you need to do some more thinking before you begin.

If you don't have a title/theme/purpose, you need to do a little creative brainstorming using the procedures covered in Chapter 5 and accomplish some preliminary research to define your manuscript.

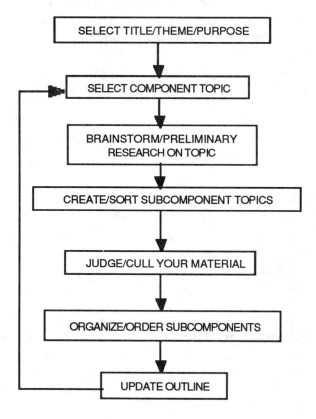

Figure 27. Universal Top-Down Subroutine

Select component topic

Next, select one component (a chapter or module) from the next level down. Using the same subroutine of Figure 27, design your lower-level components. Add this new information to update and expand your outline. Each time you step down one level, you add more details and your topics become more concrete, more definitive.

By using this modular procedure, as you continually update your outline with the new topics, you have the complete freedom to design your manuscript in any order you choose and still achieve the completeness, the logical progression of ideas or scenes, and the excellent readability that should be a part of every manuscript.

With a title/theme/purpose to serve as your guide, conduct preliminary research for this specific component (chapter or module) in sufficient detail. If you begin with a title, your preliminary research must be adequate to define your chapters for a book (or your modules for a short manuscript).

If your component is a chapter or module, you must accomplish enough preliminary research to define the components that are in the next level down, the modules for the book or the submodules for the shorter manuscripts.

Preliminary research

Two main levels of research used for writing are *preliminary* and *in-depth*. During the design phase, you need to accomplish only enough preliminary research to outline your manuscript down past the module level. Later, during the writing phase, you can conduct the in-depth research required to fill in more of the details of the modules. (In-depth is defined in Chapter 12.)

Preliminary research, also called quick and dirty research, is needed to top-down design all the way down to the topic and content of your individual chapters and modules. Preliminary research is a surface-type of investigation where you create information by brainstorming, as well as from general reference books, periodicals, general and special-topic encyclopedias, history books, novels, abstracts, directories and more.

When you conduct your preliminary research using various references, don't read all the references from cover to cover. You can obtain the essence of the references by reviewing the contents page, glancing through the index, and reading the preface and the introduction. Review the headlines in each chapter, read the first sentences in some key paragraphs and see how much emphasis the author assigned to each of these topics. Make appropriate notes using the techniques described in Chapter 7 as you conduct this research.

Brainstorming/preliminary research

Returning to the subroutine diagrammed in Figure 27, your initial efforts should be a combination of brainstorming and library research. Unless you really know your subject in considerable detail, as may be true in some fiction, you'll need the help of many references and the collective viewpoints of several authors in tentatively planning your components.

Keep in mind that the top-down design you're accomplishing here is still tentative and will remain tentative for some time. You may start out with 10 chapters (or four modules for a short). Then, as you research, you decide that one chapter (or module) should be expanded into two chapters. A different chapter can be combined with another chapter (or module), and a new chapter (or module) may have to be added later to fill a gap in your top-down design. Keep updating your outline as you do this and you'll be able to spot missing topics, combine related topics, add new topics.

This continual updating is precisely a major reason why I strongly recommend the use of a good supply of index cards for recording notes, ideas, thoughts, references, etc. Index cards are sturdy, easy to manipulate, rearrange, combine, group and regroup, time and time again, until you're satisfied with their order. Then, even if things change later, you can easily reorder, add to, revise, combine, and delete cards to obtain the end result you want.

When you brainstorm your topics, and when you conduct your library and online research, do not initially be concerned with the rank and importance of the material you're accumulating. Amass all your relevant material, whether it's for a major topic, a minor heading, an idea for a scene or a sequel, a chapter heading, a new character, a short note, some data, a xerox copy...whatever. Once you have collected all the information you need to write a specific module, you can then evaluate, order, and rank your information. However, to sort your data it's necessary to first explore the "relationships" among your material.

Ordering sequences and relationships

Topics that are *related* to each other are much more easily understood and recalled than *non-related* topics. The human mind is very good, even insistent on searching for order and logic, on recognizing patterns. For example, this list of related items:

book, pamphlet, novel, Bible

is much easier to understand and remember than this list of unrelated items:

red, television, automobile, gin

The basic "Principle of Relationships:" All topics on the same level (chapters, modules, paragraphs, etc.) must be related to each other by *one, and only one*, of the ordering relationships (time, space, etc.) described in Chapter 2. To summarize:

- **Chapter to chapter.** Same ordering sequence
- **Module to module.** Same ordering sequence within a given chapter, but can differ from one chapter to another
- **Submodule to submodule.** Same ordering sequence within a given module, but can differ from one module to another.

With this background, you are now ready to continue your top-down design of your book or article or story by

researching each module to obtain the topics and information needed to fill out a book or an article.

Create/sort subcomponent topics

Again returning to the universal top-down design subroutine of Figure 27, to create your chapter divisions and
titles (or your module divisions for a short manuscript),
you have to expand your overall purpose/premise/theme.
For this important step, conduct enough additional preliminary research and/or more creative brainstorming to
expand your manuscript idea in sufficient detail so you
can divide your subject into a number of parts. You will
need to generate a purpose/premise/theme, along with a
title, or a combination of them, for each individual chapter
(or module). Also keep in mind that when you divide the
subject of your manuscript into chapters (or modules), the
subject should be divided into topics of approximately
equal size and of roughly equal importance.

The technique I use is to conduct my brainstorming
and my preliminary research for the entire manuscript
over a period of time. It may take hours, or it may be
accomplished over a period of days, or even weeks. I make
notes on my 3-by-5 cards and accumulate them during
multiple and varied brainstorming and research sessions.
I don't worry about whether my notes are relevant, duplicate, expressed in proper grammar, or even nudge the
Richter Scale. I just write down all of my thoughts and
research notes on a topic without judging them. Finally I
reach a point where I am either saturated on a topic or
feel that I have enough information to begin with.

Next I find a large, flat surface (often the floor of my
living room or a big table) and sit down with my deck of 3-
by-5s. Typically for a book I may have accumulated 100 or
more cards with notes on them that must be sorted into
related topics and used to begin to create some chapters.

My cards are not in any particular order at this time,
so I begin with the top card and lay it, face-up, on the
surface to begin my first column. Then I study the second
card and see if it is associated with the first card in one of

the three (another Magic Three) ways established so many years ago by Aristotle. Association automatically gears imagination to memory and makes one idea lead to another. Here are Aristotle's three laws of association of ideas:

1. Is it a similar topic?
2. Is it a contiguous topic?
3. Is it a contrasting topic?

Similarity means that the topics are alike, but are not exactly the same. Apples and pears are both fruits, but they are not exactly the same. Men and women are similar, but they are not the same.

Contiguous means the topics are neighbors, joined, close together, or adjoining. One example of contiguity of topics is the tackle and guard on a football team, they have adjoining positions on the line. Another example of contiguity is love and devotion.

Contrasting means one topic is the opposite of another topic. As an example, a skyscraper and a cabin are contrasting topics, as are love and hate.

These are very important subjective judgements that shouldn't be accomplished without considerable pondering, so take your time in this important step.

To continue the sort, if the topic of my second card is associated with my first card by one of the three categories above, I place it in the same column and below the first card. If it is not associated, I place the second card in a position to start a second column. Again, don't be too concerned about getting everything perfect the first time. You move the cards around later when you see how the outline shapes up.

Next I pick up the third card and make the same comparison. If it passes one of the three tests and is associated with the first and/or second card, place the third card in the appropriate column. Continue through the deck until you have laid all the cards down and lined them up in the various columns. You should now have anywhere from five to 20 or more columns of cards, where each column is the basic content of a chapter or a module.

Now, with all of the cards placed in the columns, you have a rough outline of some of the topics your manuscript will cover. The topics are not in order yet and there are probably some duplications. Review what you have, and eliminate duplications or combine them onto a single card. You may also have some second thoughts about which column the various cards belong in. You may also want to break up or combine some columns, so do that.

Judge/cull

You were initially encouraged to accumulate much more material than you would be able to use for your topics, and to do this without judging them. Now it's time to judge your material, to separate the diamonds from the zircons. As you review your 3-by-5 cards ask these questions of each card:

- Is it a duplicate? (If so, discard it)
- Does it belong in this column? (If not, set it aside)
- Is it relevant? (If not, discard it)
- Should it be combined with others? (if so, do it)

Don't judge too harshly at this point, you'll have ample opportunity later to further judge and cull your material. Just separate the big chunks of glass at this point. If you have doubts about whether a specific topic should be used, leave it in for now; you may find a home for it later.

Organize/order

Once you are fairly satisfied that your cards have been sorted properly, take one column (one stack of cards) at a time and conduct a P-Sort to organize the cards for each individual column. When you have ordered all of the cards in the columns, review each column and create a title or note that describes the content of that specific column. It may be a tentative title for a chapter or a short description of the contents of the column. Write that title or note on a new 3-by-5 card, stack the cards from that column up in order and place the title card on top. You then have a stack of cards for a given chapter or module and a title on top that describes what that chapter or module will cover. Finally, place a rubber band around the column deck of cards to keep them in order.

Repeat this procedure for each of the other columns. You should end up with somewhere between five and 20 or more stacks of cards, each with a title or note card on top. Each stack of cards forms the elemental basis for a chapter or a module.

The next task is to use the P-Sort to organize all the individual stacks into the desired order. Go through each stack, one at a time, and order them. When this is accomplished, you have the basis for an outline that has been designed from the top down.

Update outline

Finally, input all the information from the cards into your word processor in the proper order and print it out for review. You should then review this rough outline to see if any topics are missing, which should be combined, or which should be divided up.

Again I must stress that top-down design of a manuscript is a continual iterative process. A manuscript doesn't grow in a straight line from the kernel of an idea to an accomplished fact. There are many detours, much retracing of your paths on the way. But, in writing a manuscript, as in life, it's the journey that's the most exciting, not the destination.

Another method you might consider using is to break the topic of your manuscript up into chapters (or modules) by assuming that you're going to teach a course covering the entire topic of your manuscript. Divide your topic up into 10 to 12 lectures (four to eight modules for a short seminar) and decide what you would cover in each of the lectures to teach your topics to a diverse group of students.

Repeat subroutine for all components

This same, basic subroutine should be used repeatedly to create an outline covering all the other components. For a book, you should repeat the procedure down to the module and possibly down to the submodule level for each chapter. For a short, such as an article or short story, perform the subroutine repeatedly down to the module, submodule, and down to the note level for the submodule.

Next, we'll top-down design a short story and an article using the subroutine presented in this chapter.

Exercises

1. Select a title for a short story or an article. Conduct enough preliminary research to have at least 12 events or topics in your list.
2. Order the topics/events and create a mini-outline for the short story/article.

Chapter 10

Top-down Design for a Short Story or Article

*"In whatever paragraphs or essays you write,
verify the sequence of ideas and take out or
transpose anything that interrupts the
march of thought and feeling."*
Jacques Barzun
Simple and Direct

This chapter illustrates the application of a universal subroutine for creating, planning, and organizing the material for a "short," such as short story, an article, or any of the shorter manuscript formats.

Fiction subroutine

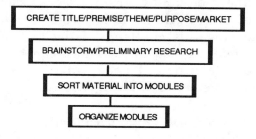

Figure 28. Top-Down Design Subroutine, Creating a Short

Figure 28 diagrams the subroutine required to top-down design the modules that comprise a short story or any short-fiction manuscript. For fiction, a module is a scene or a sequel (I'll use scene).

A short story

To demonstrate the use of the universal subroutine for writing a short story, I'll include an original one I brainstormed for this book. I usually like to begin a story idea with a theme or purpose.

We all have our own themes we feel strongly about. One of my favorite themes is when a little guy (or gal) is set upon and taken advantage of by a big guy (or gal). The big guy can be a bank, a boss, a company, a lover, a government bureaucracy, or even a computer; whatever it is that can stymie and frustrate the little guy. Because we're living in a computer age, I'll let my guy be frustrated by the overuse and abuse of automation, as so many people are in today's world.

Computers are a marvelous invention, but like so many good things, their application can be overdone. So this story will be about a computer that is used to an excess. My theme will be the little guy versus the big guy. I don't have a title yet, one will probably pop up as I brainstorm.

Brainstorming a short story

I jump-started my brainstorming session by writing the word "paper," on a 3-by-5 card, because some computer fanatics claim we will soon be working in paperless offices. Accepting this challenge, I decided to show how such an attitude, carried to extremes, can be destructive. So here are a few ideas I came up with, in a random order, to create a story to prove my theme.

- Bruno, new company president, is a fanatic who tells personnel that all paper will be eliminated in all company operations.

- Computers are installed at each desk.
- Harold, my hero, defeats Bruno the company president (I don't know how yet, but I'll come up with something later).
- Hot-air dryers are installed in the restrooms.
- Paper files are converted to computer files.
- An employee caught carrying a pad of paper and a pencil is fired.
- Harold, head of the filing department, secretly saves some key paper files.
- Bruno, suspicious of Harold, inspects Harold's office late at night and finds the hidden paper files.
- Suddenly I have my elding: A heavy, forbidden, paper-filled file cabinet falls over and pins Bruno to the floor. So the paper he hates becomes his downfall. Poetic justice! An orchestra in the distance is playing so very loudly that Bruno can't scream for help. He slowly dies as the orchestra plays, "It's Only a Paper Moon." Aha! Now there's my title, too: *"It's Only a Paper Moon."*

At this early stage of writing you should also have a market in mind since this gives you the slant you should use in your writing. For this short story, I'll direct it to the general public.

Most people's lives have been touched, and some have been harmed by automation, in various ways. So the public should be receptive to this story. And it also has a universal theme, "The little guy (comprising most of the population) versus the big guy."

Sort materials into modules

Each idea I've listed above becomes a module (which modules will be written as scenes, and which will be written as sequels can be decided later), so I have already sorted my preliminary material into modules. I didn't have to research this story because all of the ideas came from my brainstorming session, which often happens when you create fiction.

If your story requires considerable research, such as would be needed for an historical or science-fiction story, then you would have to accomplish preliminary research to accumulate enough facts and raw material to form modules and then sort the material into modules.

Organize modules

I'll use short titles to recap my modules:

- Bruno says paper no longer allowed
- Computers installed at each desk
- Harold defeats Bruno (this will be my climactic scene and is listed below, so I can eliminate this duplication)
- Hot-air dryers in restrooms
- Paper files converted to computer files
- Employee fired
- Harold secretly saves paper files
- Bruno spies on Harold's files
- Bruno dies for lack of paper and pencil

That results in eight scenes after eliminating the single duplication. In a full-blown short story I would use a few more scenes, but I've deliberately made this one short so it won't take up too much space in this chapter.

To order these scenes using the P-Sort, I'll simply list them by letter below and illustrate how I would sort them for the first round, then give you my final order.

- A. Bruno says paper no longer allowed
- B. Computers installed at each desk
- C. Hot-air dryers in restrooms
- D. Paper files converted to computer files

E. Employee fired
F. Harold secretly saves paper files
G. Bruno spies on Harold's files
H. Bruno dies for lack of paper and pencil

The P-Sort applies

To proceed with the P-Sort, each scene is written on a separate 3-by-5 card as shown in Figure 29. Compare Scene A, "Bruno says no paper" and Scene B, "Computers installed." Scene A must come first because this sets up the rest of the story, so don't interchange their order.

Next, compare Scene B "Computers installed" and Scene C, "Hot-air dryers in restrooms." I chose to let Scene C occur before Scene B because it will have an immediate and personal impact on each and every employee. So, interchange their order.

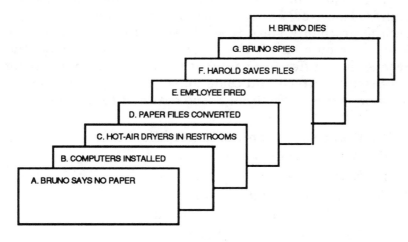

Figure 29. Cards Arranged for P-Sort

Compare Scene B "Computers installed" and Scene D, "Paper files converted." Scene B must come first since the computers must be installed before the files are converted to give the employees some experience in using computers, so don't interchange their order.

Compare Scene D, "Files converted" and Scene E, "Employee fired." I elected to have the employee fired early in the story to drive home the point that the fanatical Bruno does not care about his employees. He cares only that his paperless project succeed, so interchange their order.

Next compare Scene D, "Files converted" and Scene F, "Harold saves files." I'd like to show Harold secretly saving files before they are being converted since this is a key factor in the story's resolution, so interchange their order.

Compare Scene D, "Files converted" and Scene G, "Bruno spies." Certainly Scene G must come later, so don't interchange their order.

For the final comparison, compare Scene G, "Bruno spies" and Scene H, "Bruno dies." Scene H is the final one in the story, the resolution of the conflict, so don't change their order.

The P-Sort should then be carried through for six more rounds. However, I won't continue my example by repeating the procedure since it would take up too much space. Also, your opinion of what order should be used for the Scenes may differ from mine. (For practice, try ordering the Scenes yourself and come up with your own version of the story.) Here's the final Scene outline I came up with:

A. Bruno says paper no longer allowed
C. Hot-air dryers in restrooms
E. Employee fired
B. Computers installed at each desk
F. Harold secretly saves paper files
D. Paper files converted to computer files
G. Bruno spies on Harold's files
H. Bruno dies for lack of paper and pencil

Top-down design for an article

The subroutine for top-down design of an article is the same as for a short story. I'll repeat it here for ready reference as Figure 30. I've always been fascinated by the history of locks, so I decided to do an article about the topic. To begin my brainstorming session, I wrote the word "lock" on a 3-by-5 card to use as a jump-starter.

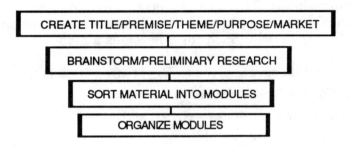

Figure 30. Top-Down Subroutine for Creating a Short

Here are some of the questions I came up with, using the "six serving men" as triggers:

- When was the first lock used?
- What kinds of locks are used
- Who used the chastity belt?
- How can combination locks be picked?
- What is the best lock for a secure home?
- How did banks fight back against the robbers?
- Where is a safe place to store valuables in your home?
- What do computer hackers do to break into computers?
- Who was Yale of the Yale lock?
- Who were some of the famous lock inventors?

Since I began with little or no knowledge of locks, I concluded my brainstorming session, not with facts, but with only a number of questions. But that's all right. These questions gave me a place and a direction to start my preliminary research.

Preliminary research

Here are a few of the specific topics I uncovered later during my preliminary research at my local library, plus the approximate time of their occurrence. Again, I'll use only the following eight topics to illustrate how to organize them for my article. Each topic becomes a module:

A. First discovered locks—Egypt circa 1000 B.C.

B. Future locks—future time

C. Combination locks—circa 1860

D. Chastity belt—Middle Ages

E. Linus Yale, lock inventor—circa 1850

F. Time locks on banks—circa 1873

G. Computer hackers—circa 1980

H. "If there is a keyhole, we can pick it." Lock picker's motto.

As I researched and reviewed my material, I concluded that what was occurring in the development of locks was a constant battle between the "haves" and the "have-nots." It was a war between the locks and the robbers. Aha! There's a possible title, "Locks and Robbers." And I could subtitle it, "The War Between the Lock-Makers and the Lock-Pickers."

Sort and organize modules

After reviewing my material, I noticed that the development of locks was actually an ongoing battle. The lock-makers would invent a supposedly secure lock, the lock-pickers would soon figure out ways to defeat it. Then the lock-makers would try again to create a secure environment, later the lock-pickers would find a way to defeat the new security measures.

So the order for presenting the material became obvious. I would use a chronological order to show how the war see-sawed back in forth in time, one battle after another. Actually the war is still going on, with the latest lock-picking being accomplished by sophisticated computer hackers picking the electronic locks of the banks, security institutions, research programs, etc.

Using the information and the P-Sort, I came up with this chronological order:

1. First locks—Egypt—circa 1000 B.C.
2. Chastity belt—Middle Ages
3. Linus Yale—lock inventor—circa 1850
4. Combination locks—circa 1860
5. Time locks on banks—circa 1860
6. Computer hackers—present time
7. Future locks—future time

Note that I didn't include the lock picker's motto because it wasn't a specific event related to a specific time as all the other modules were. However, I thought the quote would be an excellent subtitle for the article since the quote pretty much summarizes the theme of the entire piece. Note, also, that for a full-length article, I would have used at least 10 or 20 modules to provide a more continuous and more detailed chronology of the fascinating war between the locks and the robbers.

In the next chapter, the subroutine for bottom-up writing of fiction and non-fiction modules will be illustrated.

Exercises

1. Copy the events of the short story in this chapter and see if you can come up with a different order that better suits your mind.
2. Choose a subject for an article, research it, generate at least six topics and sort them using the Precedent Sort.

Chapter 11

Bottom-up Writing Subroutine for the Short

*"As for the story..., he should first sketch its
general outline and then fill in the
episodes and amplify in detail."*
Aristotle in "Poetics"

This chapter will develop the basic subroutine you can use to bottom-up write your manuscript, using the top-down designed outline created using the techniques of Chapter 9.

Why use bottom-up writing?

Not only are most things designed from the top-down, they are also built from the bottom-up. Big things are made up of little things. After a house is designed down to the smallest detail, the lumber, nails, and concrete can then be assembled to the plan that was designed and the house can be constructed from the bottom-up.

When the artwork and text are composed for an advertising program, and the detailed plans are completed, they can be assembled from the bottom-up to create a successful advertising blitz. Once the computer program is designed down to the smallest detail, the ones and zeroes can be assembled to activate the many higher and higher level subroutines needed for the complete program.

And when a manuscript is designed down to the smallest component (the module or submodule), the procedure for writing the individual modules that comprise the manuscript can begin, using and updating the detailed outline created during the top-down design phase.

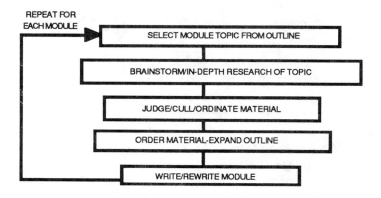

Figure 31. Bottom-Up Writing Subroutine

Select module topic from outline

To begin, select the module from the detailed outline that you feel will be the easiest to research in-depth and/or to write. It's not important whether that module is at the beginning, the middle, or the end, because a detailed outline:

- Is the glue that holds your manuscript together.
- Makes sure you cover each topic in a logical progression.
- Maps your journey from your first words, all the way to the end.

First you should accomplish the brainstorming and in-depth research required to create the detailed mountain of material needed to generate enough prose to fill each major division of your manuscript. Whether you're doing a one-chapter book (such as an article or short story) or a number of chapters for a book, it's advisable to limit your in-depth research to only one chapter or one module at a time.

Don blinders and concentrate on researching only a small part of your manuscript (a chapter or a module) so your resulting material does not become too unwieldy, too large, too confusing to manipulate.

Whichever chapter or module you choose to complete first depends on many factors. If no other reason dominates, start with the chapter or module you're most interested in. Or, if you have already accumulated considerable information on a specific chapter or module, begin with that one. Alternatively, if you intend to use one or two chapters as sample chapters in procuring a contract for a book, begin with those one or two chapters.

Brainstorming: Then in-depth research

Brainstorming was thoroughly covered in Chapter 5, and the subject of research was covered in Chapter 7. When you find yourself entrenched in either one of these processes, you may discover that it is difficult to channel all your efforts on the specific chapter or module you're working on. You'll undoubtedly accumulate considerable related information on topics that belong in other modules. Record all this information on the index cards, but at the same time refer to your top-down designed outline and note on the top of each card the chapter or module to which it belongs.

After you've accumulated a mountain of material for your specific chapter or module, it's time to critically judge that material and separate the weeds from the roses.

Judge

Earlier you were encouraged to let your creativity flow unfettered, unfenced, unbiased while you were creating.

Then you researched to verify facts, to expand your material, to answer questions, and to make notes without questioning the worth of your information. Now it's time to do that judging, to critically and objectively evaluate your ideas.

Don't be reluctant to reject some of your ideas, because eliminating superfluous ideas can tighten and make your manuscript shine brighter. Think of those superfluous ideas you have to reject as catalysts that inspired you to sprout the good ideas. Self criticism should be constructive. Don't let self criticism hold you back from making the proper, objective decisions.

To begin, find a nice, large, clutter-free, flat surface such as a large table, or the floor of a living room or other area. Lay all your cards for one chapter or one module down face up, and aligned in one or more vertical columns. This lets you view all of them, quickly compare the topics and check them for relevance to the topic.

At one side, place the card with the chapter or module title on it and line up all the cards with the module or sub-module titles face up in a vertical column under the chapter or module title card.

Cull them out

Review your cards and eliminate any that are duplicated (you'll probably find some). Next, check to see if the information on some cards overlaps. If so, combine the information on one card and discard the surplus one, or staple the two together. Then go through each card to determine its relevance to your article, If not, discard it.

You may have to go through your notes a number of times to make these decisions. If you are not certain of any note's applicability, leave it in. Err on the side of having too much information, rather than too little.

If, as you read a note, you decide that the information on the card belongs in another chapter or module, set the card aside. Mark the correct chapter number on it and save it until you start on that chapter.

Ordinate

Ordination is the process of ranking the topics by determining whether the note you have is important enough to be a chapter, or a module, or a submodule (one or more paragraphs within a module). The next step is to divide the material into these three categories.

The reason for the chapter category is that you may find that one or more of your notes do not belong in any of the chapters you've created so far and you may have to create one or more chapters to accommodate those additional topics.

Review each card individually. As you do, answer this question about each card: "Does this topic rate being a chapter, or a module, or a submodule?" These are important subjective judgments that you must make for each of your cards. This is one of the most important of all the steps because it determines how much text, how much emphasis you're going to assign to each topic, and which topics are going to be included.

Again, this is only a tentative decision since you can iterate and rearrange the cards as many times as required to achieve the desired organization.

When you make a tentative decision about each card, write an "s" on top of the card if you decide the topic is important enough to a submodule, an "m" if you decide it is worthy of being a module heading, and a "c" if it is important enough to warrant devoting an entire chapter to it. When you've finished with all the cards, set any new chapter cards aside and line up the module (or submodule) cards for the chapter or module you're working on across your surface as illustrated in Figure 32.

Next, go through the cards that have been designated as suitable for being a submodule and sort these out under the appropriate module using the three tests described in Chapter 9. I'll repeat them here for ready reference:

1. Is it a similar topic?
2. Is it a contiguous topic?
3. Is it a contrasting topic?

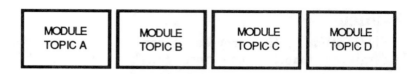

Figure 32. Arrangement of Modules

If you find one or more submodules that do not belong in one of the existing modules, and if you're sure those submodules still belong in this chapter, create one or more modules for these submodules.

Order material with the P-Sort

Now you should have all of the material for a given chapter or module sorted out. The next step is to order the material for each individual module using the P-Sort. Once you have all the modules for a given chapter organized, you now have the basic outline for that chapter.

Be sure to update your outline when you have finished sorting and ordering your information. Input the outline for each chapter into your word processor (or type it up) as soon as you complete the P-Sort for that chapter or module. Then review a printout of your outline for the chapter or module to make sure it all flows nicely from topic to topic.

At this point you can see the overall "picture" of your manuscript. Check for missing or redundant topics. Check the ordination. When you make this review, you'll probably see some duplication and find some topics that are missing. Revise your outline as necessary and do any added research you need to fill in the missing or inconsistent areas. Invest all the time you can on creating a complete, detailed, logically organized outline.

Write module

The next few modules of this text will discuss a general procedure for bottom-up writing of the text for all the modules. When it's time to write the text for the module you've selected, you'll quickly see how valuable a detailed outline is. A thorough, detailed outline shows that most of your research and creative thinking about the subject has already been accomplished.

Most of your information has been researched, collected, interpreted, and interrelated. Writing then becomes primarily a matter of developing your ideas with explanations, discussions, analogies, examples, and conflicts, and of tying them together with the necessary transitions.

With your outline completed and with the illustrations you're going to use roughed out, you're ready to write a rough draft of the selected module. And it should be considered a rough draft, because you should not at this stage be concerned with the niceties, the finer points of grammar for your first draft.

For your rough draft, don't be overanxious about the mechanics of writing. Be more concerned with the content. Concentrate on getting the information down, in the proper order, and complete.

I find that it's best to select and write one module at a time. A chapter is too big an entity to write all at once, a submodule is too short. To begin, pick the module you're most interested in. It may also be the module you have the most information about.

When you begin writing you'll discover that a significant advantage of using an outline is that you will be writing about, and concentrating on, only one module at a time. Your mind need not wander from one module to another, worrying and wondering what module to write next. You can mentally set aside all the other modules in your document for the moment and focus your total faculties on the single module you're writing.

Here we'll cover a method I've developed in writing hundreds of reports, proposals, technical articles, and five non-fiction books. This technique will take you through the steps of bottom-up writing, and revising your manuscripts. After you've tried this proven technique, you'll never need another. It makes fleshing out the text of a module easy, fast, thorough, efficient, gratifying.

Take the printout of your outline and post it up where you can see it. And if you have any illustrations roughed out, post them up also. The index cards are wonderful for taking notes and for doing the organizing, but they are not a compact method for handling, massaging, and reviewing the complete outline.

Writing the body

Follow the steps listed below in writing the body of your manuscript. It's a proven formula that will help you create a well-written manuscript, with minimal effort.

1. Get ready to bottom-up write. Find a quiet place where you won't be disturbed. Pick a time of day when your mental equipment works the best. Use a deserted office, or find a quiet room at home. Sit down and concentrate. Review and read and re-read your index card notes, all the notes for the module you've chosen. Use earplugs if you need them for this important period. This is the *single most important step* in the preparation of your manuscript, so spend some time reading, reviewing, questioning, checking and double-checking your references, all your notes for this module. You want this information to sink deeply into your mind.

2. Take a break. This next step is also very important. Once your review has been completed, put your notes aside and go off for a while and do something else, something totally unrelated to your manuscript. This gestation period is necessary so that the material you just studied can settle deep in your mind and let that marvelous, magical, mental mechanism, your subconscious, go to work on the material and sort, evaluate, add to, classify, organize, expand and rearrange.

3. Write as fast as you can. After you've been away from your material for sometime, find another quiet place and get your equipment ready. Sit down in front of your word processor, your typewriter, or your dictating machine if you're so inclined, or get a supply of pencils or pens and loose-leaf paper, and get ready to write. Tack your working outline and any illustrations you're going to use up on the wall. Or, if you're using a word processor, call up and display your outline on the video screen.

Don't consult your detailed notes, your photocopies, your cards under any circumstances at this point. This is very important! Seal your detailed notes in an envelope if you must, but *do not* look at them now. The problem with writing directly from notes is that you'll simply copy your notes directly into your text and you'll end up with a compilation of undigested facts. You'll be using the exact words from your notes, instead of putting all the information, all your thoughts and ideas into your own words. That's why doctoral theses are so unreadable because they're written directly from notes. It's better to put your individual creativity to work and write using only your working outline and visuals to guide the words from your subconscious to the keys.

Write or type as fast as you can, referring to the outlines and illustrations as you do so. Don't let anything slow down your creative process. Double or triple-space your writing or typing. You'll need this space later for corrections, additions, etc. Don't pay any attention to grammar, spelling, sentence structure, variety or length. Don't pause to make any corrections. Use incomplete sentences if you must.

Just record the words and ideas. Thoughts are associative. One thought leads to another. You must allow your thoughts to flow freely and use the style and vocabulary that are natural to yourself. If you're stuck for data, a detail, a name, a number, leave a blank space, a question mark. You can fill in the details later.

Don't let anything sidetrack you in this highly creative process. Get it all down as fast as you can. You'll find that your enthusiasm will grow once you surmount the initial hurdle of starting. You'll be amazed and pleased at how quickly thoughts come to you. Your hands will not be able to keep up with your brain. Words, thoughts, sentences will pour out of you in a logical sequence, forming a smooth-flowing narrative that you'll be proud to have authored. As you finish each submodule, cross it off your outline. If you get stuck on a particular submodule, switch to another submodule.

4. Check against your detailed notes. Soon after you've finished writing the rough draft of this module, unseal the envelope with your detailed notes in it. Read through your notes once again to see if you've left anything out. You probably have, so fill in the blanks left open in your important first draft. If you're writing by hand or typing and have left out quite a bit and have to add a page between pages 2 and 3, number it 2a. That's the beauty of using individual sheets of paper, you can easily add, subtract, reorganize as required. In a word processor you can easily insert whatever information you left out, whatever corrections you have to make. If you're dictating, you'll have to have a rough draft typed first and mark it up.

5. Review. Before reviewing the module you just completed, pause a few hours (or longer if your deadline permits it) to let your writing "cool off." "Write in haste, polish at leisure" is good advice. Then, don your editorial hat and go through what you've written, from beginning to end. Check the sentence length, structure, grammar, punctuation, spelling. If your word processor has a spelling program, use it. The speller will catch many of the mistakes you'd miss on a visual check. If you have a grammar checking program, use this also to review what you have written.

Writing requires two distinct and separate mental attitudes. When you first write about a topic, you write creatively, using the creative/intuitive part of your brain, con-centrating on getting the proper information down, in the correct order, in your own individual style.

Next, you put the logical/rational part of your brain to work and become an editor. You can't accomplish both of these separate and distinct processes at the same time, because if you pause to edit when you write your initial draft, your creative processes will be distracted, stifled, slowed down, side-tracked. Your mind will have to continually shift back and forth. This mind-jerking strips your mental gears and ruins the writing process since creativity must exist without knowing any bounds, any rules. Creativity can't be tied down, restricted by grammar.

Editing, however, is less of a creative task, but is a vital one. Pruning the branches of a fruit tree strengthens the tree and yields bigger, healthier fruit. Pruning your prose yields a stronger, more coherent manuscript.

Editing applies certain established, well-proven rules that have become accepted over the years. For this step, read your module through, from beginning to end, blue pencil (or pen) in hand, and make any needed corrections you find. If you're working with a word processor, you may prefer to edit your text on the video screen by scrolling through the text or by reviewing a printout (I prefer to use a printed copy because I can flip back and forth to double-check and compare with other parts of the manuscript). Write notes to yourself on the screen, or on the printed copy about what to do later, but don't interrupt your reading too long during this process. Read the entire draft through, at a leisurely pace to make sure the logic flows properly and the text is complete.

6. Revise. A few hours, or some time later, take the necessary time to accomplish the detailed rewrite, the additions, the corrections required. Put the spelling checker and grammar checker to work if you have them. Use the electronic or manual cut-and-paste to restructure your manuscript as you noted in Step 5 above. Because second and third thoughts are often clearer than first thoughts, revision can make the difference between a mediocre manuscript and an excellent one. And revision is made much easier when you're word processing. If you're working with a WP, it's best to perform this revision step with a printout of your entire manuscript, because all of your errors will show up better on paper and you can easily jump back and forth to check and verify the presence or absence of other topics in a printout.

Repeat for each module

Next, repeat the above procedure for a different module. The next module may be in the same chapter, or in a different chapter. Check your detailed outline to decide which module you'd like to write next.

As for my own procedure, I try to work with a given chapter and complete most of the modules in that same chapter because my mind has been conditioned to focus on the topics of that chapter. But experiment with different procedures and use whichever one is optimum for you. Remember that your outline is the road map for your journey and you won't get lost by following your outline.

Create transitions

Once you have completed all or most of a chapter, check to see if the module-to-module transitions are smooth. Module-to-module transitions in nonfiction can often be accomplished by the use of a bold heading that introduces the next topic. This is adequate if the change in topics is not too great. If the change is considerable, write a transitional sentence at the end of the first module that introduces the next module and shows how the topic of the first module ties into the topic of the next module.

In fiction, headings are not normally used. Transitions between scenes and sequels are often handled simply by double-spacing between the end of one fiction module and the beginning of another. If a considerable elapse in time or a change in place has occurred between modules, an introductory sentence in the first paragraph of the second module should be included to help the reader over this change in time and/or place. Stating the new time is often a good transition because time is usually the basis for continuity in fiction. "An hour later..." or "The next morning..." can help orient the reader for the next module or scene.

Review/revise/refine

"Of every four words I write, I strike out three."
Nicolas Boileau, French Poet, Critic

Don't worry about revising your manuscript to the extent that Boileau did, but you can see how important professional writers regard the review and revision of their manuscripts. Effective revision can elevate a so-so manuscript into a memorable one.

Again, if possible, set your manuscript aside for a few more hours or days if possible. Then read it through, from beginning to end, and make another set of corrections. Check your sentence lengths. Your average sentence length should be less than 20 words, 17 is ideal. For a quick visual check, a type-written copy usually has 10 to 12 words per line, so your average sentence length should be less than two type-written lines. Check for long words. Long words are usually abstract words. Replace them with concrete words whenever possible.

At this point you can easily see the advantages and importance of creating a detailed outline before you start writing. With the well-planned outline you've generated so far, you can begin with any module or chapter of your book, skip around in any way that is best for you, and still feel confident that all of the topics in the outline will be covered, and no topics will be omitted.

Whether you should review and revise your manuscript each time you rough-draft a module, or a chapter, or at the other extreme, wait until the entire manuscript is completed, depends on the type of material you're dealing with, the time schedule you're working to, and your personal preferences.

As for my personal preferences, I continue to outline and make notes and corrections, additions, deletions to my detailed outline as long as possible. I force myself to work at the outline and note level until I feel I am stagnating. When I get to that the point, I have to start writing.

But I don't like to revise when I write my important first draft. I usually write as fast as I can, all the way to the end of a module if I can so as not to interrupt my chain of thought. Once a module is completed, I look it over quickly to see if there are any obvious mistakes or omissions, correct them, then go on to another module.

Only after I have completed a number of modules or possibly an entire chapter, do I then go through and review what I have written. This first review is more for continuity and obvious mistakes, and checking for omissions than for any other reason.

Once a chapter is completed, I set it aside and move on to another chapter. Or I may jump from a module in one chapter to a module in another chapter when inspirations strike me. With a good outline, I know exactly where to jump and how to make the appropriate additions.

Experiment with various methods to see which suits your particular mode of working. My only caution is not to become too concerned with grammar, sentence construction, or spelling in the early parts of your rough drafts because it ties your creative muscles in knots.

The next chapter will show how these procedures are applied in the bottom-up writing of a portion of the short story and a portion of the article that were created in Chapter 10. One module will be bottom-up written for the short story and one for the article.

Exercises

1. Brainstorm to expand one of the topics/events of the short story or article outlined in Chapter 11 to obtain at least a dozen subtopics/subevents.
2. Order these subtopics/subevents using the Precedent Sort.
3. Write one module for your short story/article using the subtopics/subevents created in Exercise 1.

Chapter 12

Bottom-up Writing: Two Examples

"Don't write merely to be understood. Write so you cannot possibly be misunderstood."
Robert Louis Stevenson

This chapter will take the outlines that were top-down designed in Chapter 9 and show how to bottom-up write a typical module for both the short story and the article .

To refresh your memory, I'll repeat the overall short story outline designed and organized in Chapter 9:

A. Bruno says paper no longer allowed
C. Hot-air dryers in restrooms
E. Employee fired
B. Computers installed at each desk
F. Harold secretly saves paper files
D. Paper files converted to computer files
G. Bruno spies on Harold's files
H. Bruno dies for lack of paper and pencil

Applying the principles of modular writing, I chose module H as the module I felt I would most enjoy writing first. I had some special ideas for this final module of the story. Sometimes it's a good procedure to write the final fiction scene or sequel first so that everything that happens earlier can be planted, will point to, and be justified by this climactic scene. Here are, in the random order I conceived them, my topics from brainstorming and researching Module H in-depth:

1. Harold keeps carrier pigeon in his file room.
2. Harold uses carrier pigeon to send messages to his mother when he's working late because his boss refuses to let his employees make personal calls.
3. As Bruno lies dying, the carrier pigeon lands on him, and coos, apparently eager to deliver a message.
4. In the distance an orchestra is playing, "It's Only a Paper Moon."
5. Bruno searches frantically and finally finds Harold's hidden paper files.
6. Safe falls on Bruno.
7. Bruno cannot find paper and pencil.
8. Late at night Bruno sneaks into Harold's office to search to see if Harold is following the new paperless rules.

Judge/ordinate/cull module material

After reviewing what I had brainstormed, I judged and culled my material, combined, and ordinated the topics and came up with this revised list of events for this fiction module:

1. Harold keeps carrier pigeon in his office to send messages to his mother when he's working late because his boss refuses to let employees make personal calls.
2. As Bruno lies dying, the carrier pigeon lands on him, and coos, apparently eager to deliver a message.

3. In the distance an orchestra is playing, "It's Only a Paper Moon."
4. Bruno searches frantically and finally finds Harold's hidden paper files.
5. Safe falls on Bruno.
6. Bruno cannot find paper and pencil.
7. As Bruno is dying he remembers that his daughter had asked him to buy her some paper dolls and he had refused.
8. Bruno heads for Harold's office to search for forbidden paper.

Note that I not only combined and simplified my notes, I also created another note, adding note 7. Remember that your writing keeps changing as you brainstorm, research, outline, and write.

Lest the reader feel too sorry for Bruno, let me assure you that I would paint him as the despicable character he is in the early scenes and sequels, firing people with many years of seniority without warning, cutting salaries, establishing restrictive rules, cutting fringe benefits, basically emasculating the company.

Order module material

Using the P-Sort, I ordered the material and came up with this outline:

8. Bruno heads for Harold's office to search for forbidden paper.
4. Bruno searches frantically and finally finds Harold's hidden paper files.
1. Harold keeps carrier pigeon in his office to send messages to his mother when he's working late because his boss refuses to let employees make personal calls.
5. Safe falls on him.
2. As Bruno lies dying, the carrier pigeon lands on him, apparently eager to deliver a message.

6. Bruno cannot find paper and pencil.
7. As Bruno is dying he remembers that his daughter had asked him to buy her some paper dolls and he had refused.
3. In the distance an orchestra is playing, "It's Only a Paper Moon."

Write/revise/refine module text

"Nothing is really written until it is published."
Stanley Vestal

I decided to write this module as a scene because it will be filled with conflict. Using the material I brainstormed above, here's my climactic scene:

The building was quiet, deserted as Bruno hurried down the hall, his excitement rising as he pondered the delicious thought of discovering what the non-conformist Harold was secretly plotting to do to wreck his paperless office plan. Everyone had already gone home on schedule more than three hours earlier. A few weeks earlier Bruno had fired all the security guards and installed an automated, fool-proof, burglar alarm system, saving the company many thousands of dollars a year in salaries and fringe benefits. So he was completely alone in the entire building.

His hands trembling in anticipation, Bruno unlocked the door at the end of the hall that led to Harold's huge file room. He stepped in, paused a moment and studied the beautiful laser readers he had installed to replace Harold's ugly old-fashioned file cabinets.

All efficient, totally automated laser readers, standing tall in the middle of the room, the very latest in automation. "How beautiful they look," he thought. What a genius he was to think that he had replaced all those heavy, cumbersome, manual file cabinets with a few laser disks and some laser-disk changers to quickly access all the files that were now stored on the disks. All a user had to do was request the file and it was instantly delivered to his computer terminal, without requiring a single piece of paper.

These machines are definitely the answer to the future, he nodded in satisfaction. They don't get angry, or tired, or lazy. Their feelings don't get hurt. They don't go on strike. There is no quota system to hassle with. They don't demand vacations, nor fringe benefits, nor sick leave. They can slave 24 hours a day, seven days a week, without demanding any overtime pay. "Yep," he smiled, "I sure made the right decision here."

Beginning his search, he looked in every corner of Harold's file room, peered under the laser readers, dug back in the shelves. He ransacked Harold's desk, but could find nothing suspicious.

Disappointed, he plopped down in Harold's swivel chair and scanned the room. Suddenly he stopped. He hadn't noticed it before, but there was a big closet in the far corner of the room. "Bet that old codger's got something hidden in there," he said, jumping up.

But the door to the closet was locked. Hurrying back to Harold's desk, he searched but was unable to find any keys. After locating a large screwdriver in the bottom drawer, he snatched it up, strode over to the closet, slipped the screwdriver into the door frame, and popped the door open.

"Why that old traitor!" Bruno gasped, stumbling back as he studied the eight-foot tall, heavy-steel, forbidden filing cabinet that filled the entire closet.

His excitement rising, Bruno stepped forward and jammed the screwdriver into the bottom drawer of the file and forced it open. "Paper!" he spit out the hated word as he spotted a huge pile of paper files stacked in the drawer. He broke open two other drawers and almost gagged as he saw the hundreds of paper files crammed inside. "That little midget's been breaking all my rules," he said, kicking the file cabinet. "Wait until I see him in the morning. I'm not even going to give him five min - utes notice to clear the hell out of my building!"

"Wonder what's in that top drawer," he pon- dered, then walked over to pull Harold's swivel chair over for a look at the high drawer he couldn't reach. The chair was unsteady as he stepped up on it and he nearly fell.

"Coo! Coo!" a sound came from the top of the cabinet.

Bruno looked up. "Damn him! That old man still has his stupid homing pigeon here! I warned him two months ago that his Dickie bird had to go." Reaching up, Bruno snatched the bird cage and held it up in front of him. He glared at the pigeon in the cage, then began to laugh so hard that his entire body shook.

Suddenly the wheels of the swivel chair started to turn and the chair started to roll away from the cabinet. To prevent his fall, Bruno flung the bird cage aside and grabbed on to the heavy file cabinet. But Bruno's weight was too great and the cabinet, heavily unbalanced with its paper-filled drawers open, started to fall toward him. Frantic, he tried to jump out of the way, but the loss of his footing threw him completely off-balance and he fell, slamming hard against the floor, banging his head on the side of the nearby laser reader. The heavy file cabinet crashed down on top of him, crushing him to the floor.

Moments later he shook his head, feeling weak. The cabinet had him completely pinned to the floor. He couldn't move.

"Help! Help!" he shouted weakly in his panic, but there was no one in the plant to hear him. In the distance he heard a loud radio playing music.

"If I could only reach that stupid phone!" he cried out. He struggled with all his might, but couldn't budge the heavy, steel, paper-filled cabinet.

As he lay on the floor, imprisoned under the heavy cabinet, he glanced down at his side. A pool of blood was collecting. He felt the strength slowly draining out of his body.

"Coo! Coo!" The cry made Bruno jerk his head. It was Harold's pigeon, Dickie. The cage had broken open when he had tossed the cage aside. Harold's pigeon strutted around the room, sticking its chest out. "Coo! Coo!"

"Here, nice little pigeon, here Dickie bird, nice birdie!" Bruno called out, but the homing pigeon ignored his command.

"If I only had a piece of paper and a pencil. I could write a note and tie it to Dickie bird's leg. Then he could fly to Harold's home and bring me help."

He sighed aloud. He had no paper. He had no pencil.

Dickie cooed and cooed and came closer and closer to Bruno. "Damn you!" he swore at the pigeon.

Bruno kept talking out loud, struggling to keep from losing consciousness. "I just remembered," he sighed. "My wife asked me to buy her some stationery this morning. And I refused. And my little girl wanted me to buy her some paper dolls. I refused her, too."

Slowly the strength drained from Bruno's body as he lay on the floor. He struggled, but couldn't move. Blood continued to flow out of the gash in his side.

In the distance he heard the sound of the loud radio playing an old ballad. He could hear the words plainly. As the vocalist wailed the words of the song, Bruno felt life slowly ebbing from his body. He moaned in agony as the female vocalist sang:

"It's only a paper moon, Sailing over a cardboard sea."

THE END

As you will notice, I followed my basic outline to write this scene, but made some changes as I went along. Keep reviewing and revising until you feel comfortable and confident enough to write "The End" on your manuscript.

And now for the article

The article will be written from the bottom-up using the subroutine of Figure 33.

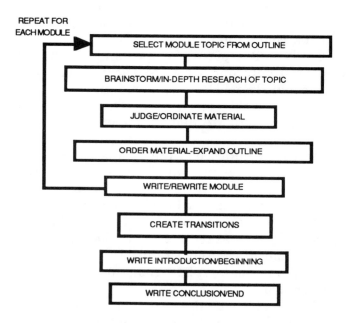

Figure 33. Bottom-Up Writing Subroutine for Article

Select module topic from outline

The module I wanted to write first was the one I was most interested in: the present-day computer hackers. This module should also make the article more topical because hackers are alive and busily picking the locks in today's computer world. So I decided to research computer hacking first. Although many computer-hacking incidents have been reported in the news-media and periodicals, I uncovered four that I found particularly interesting and researched them in depth. The titles of these four were:

A. 36-year-old mother of two heads a hacker ring
B. Robert T. Morris picks locks of computer network and slips worm through keyhole
C. Hackers at Berkeley
D. Hackers pick locks of sensitive U.S. networks

Judge/ordinate/cull

After reviewing these incidents in detail, I concluded that the story of the hacker at Berkeley was just too involved and complex to include in this article, so I culled it out. For the remaining three, I decided to begin with what I thought was the most interesting module, that of the 36-year old mother of two, then follow with the other two in chronological order. The order then became:

• 36 year-old mother of two
• Hackers pick locks of sensitive material— March 1985
• Robert T. Morris picks locks, plants worm— November 1988

Write/revise/refine module text

Using the notes I had accumulated from my detailed research on the above topics, I wrote, revised, and refined the text of the module. Here is the result:

In May 1989, Leslie Lynne Doucette, a 36-year-old mother of two, pleaded guilty in Chicago federal court to defrauding phone companies and corporations of nearly $600,000 using information stolen by breaking into the locks of computer mail systems. She headed a ring of 150 hackers, people whose specialty is to find the "keyhole" and pick the locks of computer systems. The hackers steal money indirectly by pilfering credit card numbers, long-distance telephone calling-card codes, and corporate private-branch-exchange (PBX) access codes.

Earlier, in March 1988, a group of hackers was arrested for picking the locks, via an electronic keyhole, and using overseas links to U.S. computer networks to steal sensitive data.

In November 1988, Robert T. Morris located another keyhole and picked the electronic locks of the Unix-based Internet research and defense network. He squeezed a worm through the keyhole that wriggled its way through the country-wide network and shut down more than 6,000 computers. The cost of exterminating this electronic worm was an estimated $15 million.

Although the complexity of electronic safeguards and complex locking systems continues to increase, the lock-pickers always seem to be only a half-step behind in locating the keyholes.

After repeating the write/revise/refine process for all the modules, you need to create transitions. For the module-to-module transitions in an article, the use of bold headings often suffices if there is not too great a jump in subject matter. For this story on locks, headings are adequate because the tale is told in pretty much an easy-to-follow, sequential time order. So I could then use headings for each module to serve as transitions.

Write introduction/beginning

Because I wanted this article to be topical and to appeal to the general public, I decided to begin the article with the most interesting module, a hook to entice the reader into reading the entire article. So I decided to use the module I had just written on computer hacking as my introduction.

Write conclusion

For the conclusion I needed to try to come to some kind of resolution to the continuing war by examining a number of possible solutions to achieve unpickable locks. Some that came to mind were:

- Program a lock so that only specific individuals fingerprints would open the lock (Counterpoint—To "pick" this lock a crook would only have to force, under threat of death, an approved person to open the lock.)
- Develop more sophisticated access procedures for computers (Counterpoint—The bad guys can be as smart as the good guys and would probably be able to pick any new sophisticated electronic locks.)
- Initiate severe penalties for the lock-pickers that get caught (Counterpoint—This might deter a few, but there are always enough bad guys around that will take that chance.)

Here's my short conclusion:

It's very likely that whatever method the lock-makers can come up with, the lock-pickers can pick it. It may be a problem that has no solution. The war between the lock-makers and the lock-pickers may never end.

THE END

Exercises

1. Choose a scene or sequel for a short story. Follow the subroutine of Figure 32 and write a scene or sequel for the short story.
2. Choose an article topic. Use the subroutine of Figure 32 and write a module for the article.

Chapter 13

Good
Writing
Techniques

---

*"The greatest merit of style, of course, is to
have words disappear into thoughts."*
Nathaniel Hawthorne

This chapter will show you techniques that add a
higher polish to your writing and instill in you the confidence to tackle a huge article for a first-rate periodical,
perhaps even to start working toward the ultimate goal of
most writers, a full-length book.

According to the master of style, William Strunk, Jr.,
"Vigorous writing is concise. A sentence should contain
no unnecessary words, a paragraph no unnecessary sentences, for the same reason that drawing should have no
unnecessary lines and a machine no unnecessary parts.
This requires not that the writer make all of his sentences
short, or that he avoid all details and treat his subjects
only in outline, but that every word tell."

What is good writing?

Good writing effectively communicates what the writer
has to say to the reader, with a minimum of effort on the
reader's part. Simple.

"If you would not be forgotten as soon as you are
dead, either write things worth reading
or do things worth writing."
Benjamin Franklin

Good writing uses many of the techniques you've learned throughout your life, plus what you've learned in this book and will learn in this chapter. Good writing has many ingredients. Among them are:

- Logical organization of the material
- Grammar
- Spelling
- Short sentences and paragraphs; vary their lengths

Above all, don't use big words!

"Good prose is like a window pane—the less
you're aware of it, the better."
George Orwell

Yes, good writing is "invisible." By that I mean good writing helps your reader easily understand what you've written, but does not make obvious which techniques you've used to attain this effect. Properly used, these techniques are totally transparent to your readers.

How we understand

The basic element of writing, the basic symbol that paints a picture in a reader's mind, is the *word*. But the 500 most used English words have a total of 14,000 dictionary definitions—that's an average of 28 meanings per word. And words can form radically different shades of meaning in different peoples' minds.

For example, "house" can form a picture for different people ranging from a tiny, rundown shack, to a condo, to a 50-room mansion. So you can see the importance of using the proper word.

"Broadly speaking, the short words are the
best, and the old words best of all."
Sir Winston Churchill

Groups of words (phrases and sentences) modify and clarify the intrinsic meaning of these words. Words should be used effectively to sharpen the focus of the picture they are to create. "Man" gives you an out-of-focus, fuzzy, indefinite picture. "Fat man" brings the picture a little more in focus. "Short, swarthy, grossly fat man" sharply focuses the image the words are to convey. The more specific the word, the more concrete, the sharper, and the more in-focus the picture.

Emotion in fiction

In fiction, words should not only describe action, they should also create emotion in a reader. Not only groups of words, even single words can express emotion. Dr. Wilfred Funk, lexicographer and dictionary publisher, selected the ten most expressive words in the English language. They are:

emotion conveyed	word
most bitter	alone
most reverent	mother
most tragic	death
most beautiful	love
most cruel	revenge
most peaceful	tranquil
saddest	forgotten
warmest	friendship
coldest	no
most comforting	faith

These words convey emotion; there are thousands of others. But words alone cannot completely convey the desired emotion. The order of words used is also an important part of creating emotion.

Word order

Mrs. Albert Einstein was asked one day if she understood her husband's theories. She replied, "I understand the words, but I don't always understand the sentences."

It's not only the words you use, but also the word order in your sentences that is important. Words in your sentences must be arranged so that they can mean only what is intended. In the English language, changing the word order changes the meaning:

> Man bites snake.
> Snake bites man.

The proper word order is needed to paint the precise picture you want.

Another important aspect of helping your readers understand is consecutiveness: things happen in a given order. Using the proper word order makes an idea, an instruction, an emotion, a conflict, easy to follow. Still, words are not substitutes for thoughts. You must group words together to form a sentence. But no sentence, regardless of the words you use, is any better than the thought behind it.

Vocabulary

We read in terms of words, and we understand words within the limits of our vocabulary. Unless the *message* is contained within the area of the common vocabulary shared by the writer and the reader, as shown in Figure 34, there is no communication. In addition, the words in the message must mean the same to both writer and reader.

The problem created by using big or unfamiliar words is that it forces your readers to pause and stumble in confusion in their reading. They must then consult their memories or stop and look it up in a dictionary and translate the word into a more common word that they understand. This not only requires more effort in reading your prose, it can also interrupt the chain of thought you are trying to maintain. When writing calls attention to itself, it fails.

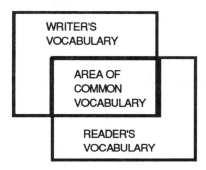

Figure 34. Writer's/Reader's Vocabularies

A large vocabulary isn't needed for effective communication. An estimated 1,000 words cover about 85% of a writer's requirements on all ordinary subjects. You can certainly do most of your writing without having to resort to long, abstract, indefinite words. If you use as many of the 1,000 basic words as you can in place of complex words or jargon, your writing will be that much easier to read, and effortless to understand.

Grammar

Proper grammar must be used to effectively communicate something to someone, not only to avoid misunderstanding, but also because your reader will notice improper grammar. Grammatical errors distract your reader's attention away from the primary purpose of your writing: communicating information.

It's no grave sin to misuse a few who's or whom's since few people understand, or even care about these finer points of grammar dreamed up by an elitist group of self-serving English teachers. But, if you make obvious mistakes, such as using the wrong tense of verbs, incorrect syntax, or order of words, or make other serious basic errors in grammatical construction, your readers are jerked away from understanding the intent of your article and they start looking for more errors in grammar. This distracts them, taking their concentration away from understanding the content.

How about spelling?

When your manuscript is sprinkled with misspelled words, your readers are again diverted from understanding the content. Also, when your audience reads a manuscript full of typos, errors, misspelled words, etc., they begin to distrust the accuracy of the content. With the variety of modern electronic dictionaries and with the excellent spelling programs now available in most word processors, spelling errors should soon become mostly a thing of the past.

Of the approximately 20,000 commonly used words, only one percent are consistently misspelled. And of these 200, the 50 that cause the most trouble are listed:

grammar	consensus	ridiculous
argument	accommodate	nickel
surprise	occurrence	oscillate
achieve	conscience	tyrannous
anoint	commitment	drunkenness
definitely	embarrass	dissension
separate	allotted	connoisseur
desirable	indispensable	sacrilegious
development	liaison	battalion
existence	proceed	prerogative
pronunciation	harass	iridescent
occasion	perseverance	inadvertent
assistant	ecstasy	genealogy
repetition	antiquated	vilify
privilege	insistent	inoculate
dependent	exhilarate	dilettante
irresistible	vacuum	

If you can study and be extra careful with these words, you'll have a good start.

Short is better

Short sentences and paragraphs have been proven to be effective ways to communicate ideas. A reader tries to comprehend an entire sentence in one gulp, looking ahead to the period (the rest period) before pausing. Avoid long, convoluted sentences. Put the main message at the front of the sentence. If your statement has to be qualified, do that in the next sentence.

Paragraphs

A paragraph is a sentence or a group of sentences that expresses and develops *one major idea*. The reader's mind is geared to reading and understanding a single idea, feeling that once a paragraph is read, the idea has been completely presented and he or she deserves a momentary pause before tackling the next idea or paragraph.

Use paragraphs of varied length. You can use this technique to highlight the more important ideas with longer paragraphs, contrasting them with shorter paragraphs that convey less important ideas.

Experience has shown that readers can grasp material most readily when it is presented in units of 75 to 200 words. With an average of 10 words per typed line, that's a range of 7.5 to 20 lines to allow per paragraph. Use some one-sentence paragraphs, some much longer. Vary their lengths for variety.

Transitions

"Word-carpentry is like any other kind of carpentry: you must join your sentences smoothly."
Anatole France

Transitions are the bridges that link paragraphs, thoughts, and ideas together. Some of the more commonly used transitions are:

- Time—Later, The next time, Finally, Next, Concurrently, After.

- Place—In the next room, Farther down the hall, At our plant in Oregon.

- Piling up of detail—And, Also, Furthermore, In addition, Moreover, Besides.

- Contrast—But, However, Though, Although, Nonetheless, Yet.

- Illustration—For example, To illustrate, In particular, For instance.

- Cause-Effect—Thus, Therefore, In conclusion, As a consequence, As a result, Consequently.

- Comparison—In a similar way, Likewise, Similarly, Here again, Consequently.

- Concession—Although, Even though, Though.

- Summary—To sum up, In brief, In short.

- Repetition—In other words, That is, As has been stated.

- Numbered or lettered steps—Used in a procedure.

- Repetition of and references to preceding ideas, key words, or phrases.

Punctuation

Punctuation is the written equivalent of the rhythm and emphasis in our speech. It takes the place of the rise and fall of our voice, the pauses and emphasis in our speech. The major function of punctuation is to make writing clearer and easier to read. Punctuation helps express, question, emphasize, surprise, conclude.

When we speak, our listeners learn as much from the *way* we speak as they learn from the *words* we speak. We gesture, screw up our face, raise or lower our voice, pause, speak fast or slow, high or low, use our hands, eyebrows, our facial expressions to add emphasis to words. In writing, our commas, our periods, our question marks and exclamation points serve as our raised eyebrows, our pauses, our shrugged shoulders.

The curse of big words

Bertrand Russell stated in his "How I Write": "Big men write little words, little men write big words."

Written ideas and concepts are difficult enough to understand without a writer complicating them even more by trying to show off his or her vocabulary. When you use such a big word as "matriculate," your readers must expend the time and the energy to translate that longer word into its simple equivalent, "enroll," before they can see the image or understand the action.

You should write to *express* not to *impress*. Even the most complex scientific ideas can be presented by simple (three-syllable or less) words. Some of the most famous and brilliant scientists of all time (Darwin, Pasteur, Madame Curie are examples) explained their complex concepts in words so simple that the public could understand and appreciate the significance of their discoveries. Undoubtedly their clear writing contributed as much to their fame as did their discoveries.

It takes a little mind (with a dictionary and a thesaurus) to write with big words. It takes a big mind to express complex thoughts and ideas in short words.

But, don't overdo it

If abused, these techniques lose their effectiveness. If you use only one or two sentences for every paragraph all through your manuscript, or 10-word "Dick and Jane and Spot" sentences, you again distract your reader from understanding the message you want to convey. The techniques of good writing should be invisible. Your reader shouldn't know what you're doing to him or her, nor how you're doing it, so they can enjoy your writing and learn from, and understand what you've written.

Anecdotes

Anecdotes, or "mini-stories" are another effective method of leading into a topic and making a point at the same time. We all like to peek into other people's lives. We learn so much by observing them. Anecdotes also add a much needed degree of informality to pedantic periodicals.

To be an effective and integral part of your manuscript, your anecdotes should relate directly to your topic by illustrating it, expanding on it, introducing it, or making a point. Anecdotes should not be dragged in simply to entertain, they should be an essential part of your presentation.

Direct quotes of well-known people, or of experts in your profession are another effective method of introducing a topic or of making a point. They are used often in this book. A study by the Kentucky Department of Communication showed that readers expressed a preference for direct quotes, rather than paraphrased statements. So when you use a quote, use a direct quote and enclose it in quotation marks.

Retention curve

One extremely important aspect of the manner in which a person's mind works is illustrated in Figure 53. This curve is valid for **all** people, of **all** cultures, regardless of education. It's a fundamental fact of human nature. Stated simply, the above curve illustrates that:

The mind remembers best what it experiences, hears, and reads first and last.

This fascinating fact holds true for a book, a movie, a speech, an article, your life's experiences...whatever you see, or hear, or read.

Your reader will best remember the beginning and ending sections the best. And that's why the Summary and Conclusions of your article, the first and last chapters of your book are worth your best efforts.

The same phenomenon holds true for both sentences and paragraphs. The first and last parts of sentences and of paragraphs are best remembered by your readers. That's why the Topic Sentence (the first sentence in your paragraph which introduces the paragraph's contents) is so important. And the final sentence of your paragraph should be a sort of conclusion, leaving your readers with the feeling of having been introduced to a concept in the first sentence and ending with understanding the idea put forth in the Topic Sentence.

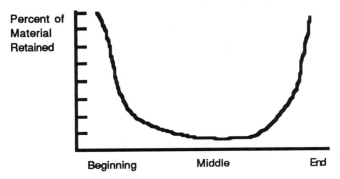

Figure 35. Retention Curve

This important aspect of the human mind is used in many, many ways, especially by astute politicians. It is an established fact that on election ballots, when a person's name is in the middle of two opponents' names, that person will lose several percentage points off his or her total vote. That is true, regardless of the candidate's qualifications. People simply vote more for the names at the top and bottom of a listing.

You can take advantage of the Retention Curve in many ways. Keep it in mind when you want to emphasize one or more points. Put the most important points in the first part of your writing, in your first paragraphs, in the first sentences of your paragraphs, and at the beginnings and endings of your sentences. And save some of your best writing for the last, the Conclusion, the final section of your article, the final chapter of your book.

You can also use the phenomenon of the Retention Curve to conceal information, bad data, meager results, etc. Bury bad information, which you must include for completeness, in the middle of a manuscript. A strong opening paragraph will often negate the bad information that may have been created by the data in the middle.

Readability

I discussed earlier that you should use short sentences and, above all, **DON'T USE BIG WORDS**. But I didn't say how short, nor how many syllables they should contain on the average.

Over the years a number of communication experts (Flesch and Gunning, for example) have developed various readability formulas. These formulas are a quantitative evaluation of a written document, showing the relative ease of reading the document. By using the number of words in a sentence and the number of syllables in the words, this formula comes up with a number called the "Readability Index." This Readability Index relates to the number of years of education a person should have to be able to read and understand a specific piece of writing.

Here are some examples:

Reader's Digest	8
Wall Street Journal	10
John Steinbeck's novels	7
Time and *Newsweek*	10

This means that the sentence length and number of syllables per sentence in *Reader's Digest*, for example, are written so they can be read and understood by a person having an eighth-grade education, and only a 10th-grade education is required for the *Wall Street Journal*. Writing communicates best when the readability level is slightly below the comprehension of the reader so your reader can enjoy your prose without having to strain for meaning or struggle with long sentences.

Fog index

The Fog Index, developed by Robert Gunning, is based on the length of words and sentences in an article. This

Index includes a factor that relates it to the approximate number of years of schooling needed to understand the prose. The higher the Fog Index, the more difficult it is to read.

Here's how to find the Fog Index:

1. Take a sample of at least 100 words. Count the number of average words per sentence. Treat independent clauses as separate sentences.

2. Count the number of polysyllables (words of three syllables or more) per 100 words. Do not count capitalized words or combinations of short, easy words such as "people-power" and verbs that are made into three syllables by adding "-es" or "-ed."

3. Add the average number of words per sentence to the polysyllable count and multiply the sum by 0.4. Ignore digits after the decimal point. If you end up with a number of over 17, you are too deep in a fog. Work your way down to a fog index of 10 or less.

An example

The best way to illustrate the above principles is by an example. Consider this sample:

In spite of the tendency of most scientific writers to use big words, even the most complex concepts can be explained in simple words. It doesn't take "big" words to explain big concepts. For example, why should a writer say that "as the temperature is elevated to the vicinity of 100 degrees Centigrade, the condition of the water becomes vaporous?" It can be phrased much simpler. "At 100 degrees Centigrade, the water turns to steam."

The Fog Index will be calculated for the sample paragraph above. The paragraph has a total of 75 words and 5 sentences or an average of 15 words per sentence. And that's 10 polysyllables or about 2 polysyllables per 100 words. The Fog Index then becomes: Fog Index = 0.4 (15 + 2) or 6.8, requiring only a seventh-grade education to understand the passage.

Whenever you find yourself shaking your head when you read something, pause for a moment and analyze it. Did the author use long sentences? Are the sentences filled with polysyllable words that boggle your mind instead of explaining?

And, when you read something easy to understand, pause a moment and analyze it also. Did the author use short and varied length sentences and simple words? Are the thoughts logically organized so that one follows the other in the proper order?

How about this book?

Just to show I practice what I preach, and also to give you a feeling of the numbers involved, I took many random samples of the writing in this book. The results are:

Average sentence length	17 words
Average word length	1.53 syllables
Reading Grade Level	11.9 years

You see that my average sentence length is 17, as recommended by the writing experts. My average word length is 1.53 syllables, which is a little below the consultants' recommendations of less than 1.68, but of course, I'm simple-minded. And my Reading Grade Level is 11.9 years, just a hair below the recommended level of 12 years.

A warning!

Please don't take these rules for sentence length and number of polysyllables as gospel. They are only intended as rough guidelines to help you check and keep a rein on your writing from time to time. They are, however, very useful to help you from becoming too pompous and long-winded.

Cliches to avoid

I'm including some of the most frequently abused cliches here:

What the writer said	What the writer should have said
The purpose of this article is	This article describes..
This report is submitted to	This report sums up..
In order to conduct	To conduct..

("In order" can be left out of all writing.)

It is recommended that the procedure should be	The procedure should be..

(Watch out for "It...that" constructions, they waste a lot of words).

It may be said that wisdom is	Wisdom is..
It is interesting to note that the document will	The document will..
In accordance with	Per..
As defined in	Per..
Shall have the capability of expanding	Shall expand..
The VCR shall be tested per	Test the VCR per..
Due to the fact that	Because..
demonstrates that there is	shows..
during such time	while..
in consideration of the fact that	if..
make an approximation as to how	estimate..
reduced to basic essentials	simplified..
would seem to suggest	suggests
for the purpose of	for, to..
is designed to be	is..
in close proximity	close to; near..
subsequent to	after..
in the event that	if..
in order to	to..
involves the use of..	employs, uses..

Exercises

1. Choose 2 or more pages of writing you have accomplished and calculate the Fog Index.
2. Calculate the Fog Index of a Reader's Digest or Wall Street Journal article.
3. Calculate the Fog Index of a leading periodical or journal in your profession or one you're interested in.

Afterword

A Little
Feedback,
Please

I have introduced a number of new and somewhat unique writing techniques in this book. My goal has been to help make both your fiction and nonfiction writing easier and more productive. Writing well is a skill that can be cultivated with proper practice and dedication. Give these techniques a trial. Adapt them to your personal rhythms. Use them to help you in all your writing efforts.

It is my sincere hope that this book has helped you on your way, no matter what type of writing you do. For few things in life can give you the satisfaction of writing and having published some memorable prose or poetry.

In our writing, as well as in our personal relationships, feedback helps us to improve. So I'd like to hear your comments, what you did and did not like, what I communicated well, what I failed to communicate properly. Just write to me and I'll use your feedback to improve future editions of this book. My mailing address is:

Harley Bjelland
P.O. Box 676
Springfield, OR 97477

May good writing flow from your creative mind and may your writing shine for all to see.

Appendix A

References
and
Sources

The following categories of reference books listed are arranged alphabetically:

- Abstracts and Indexes
- Almanacs
- Atlases
- Bibliographies
- Biographies
- Books
- Dictionaries—General
  - Abridged
  - Unabridged
- Drama
- Encyclopedias-General Interest
- Government Publications
- History
- Language—Style and Usage
- Libraries—How to Locate One
- Newspapers
- People
- Periodicals
- Publishers
- Statistics

For the reference books that follow, the title is listed first, followed by the author (if one is listed), then the publisher. A date such as (1941—) means they first published in 1941 and still are, at last report, publishing.

Abstracts and indexes

Here you'll find the most up-to-date periodical, report, and document references. All of these abstracts and indexes, plus many more, are available on the various On-Line systems.

Arts and Humanities Citation Index—Philadelphia: Institute for Scientific Information (1976—). Annual cumulation. Multi-disciplinary index to journals in the arts and humanities, indexing hundreds of journals in literature, fine arts, drama, poetry, dance, etc.

Biological Abstracts—Bio-Sciences Information Service. (1926—). Semimonthly. Worldwide reporting of research in life sciences. Principal abstracting journal for biology. Contains abstracts, author index, biosystematic index, generic index, and subject index.

Education Index—New York: Wilson (1929—). Monthly except July and August. A cumulative author, subject index of educational periodicals and yearbooks. Very useful for current information. Indexes about 325 periodicals, proceedings and yearbooks.

Engineering Index—Engineering Information Inc. (1884—). Monthly with annual accumulations. The basic English language abstracting service. Abstracts more than 2,700 professional and technical journals, as well as reports and proceedings published in 20 or more languages. A general index to engineering literature, arranged by subject, with an author index.

General Science Index (GSI)—H. W. Wilson Co. (1978—). Monthly. Indexes more than 100 general science periodicals not completely covered by other abstracts and indexes, in astronomy, chemistry, electricity, mathematics, physics, etc.

Index to Legal Periodicals—NY: Wilson (1909—). Published for American Association of Law Libraries.

Monthly index with annual cumulations. Subject author index, tables of cases, book review index. Indexes periodicals published in U.S., Canada, Great Britain, Ireland, Australia, and New Zealand.

Index Medicus—Washington National Library of Medicine (1960—). Quarterly. Contains subject, name, and bibliography of medical reviews. More than 2,000 periodicals are indexed, either completely or selectively.

Psychological Abstracts—Lancaster, Pa. American Psychological Association (1927—). Monthly. Bibliography lists new books, journal articles, technical reports, and other scientific documents with a signed abstract of each. Author and brief subject index.

Reader's Guide to Periodical Literature—H. W. Wilson (1900—). Semimonthly. Best known popular periodical index. Author and subject index to general interest periodicals (limited, however, only covers about 174 of thousands of magazines in circulation), including a few scientific periodicals published in the U.S. From 1802-1906 it was titled "Poole's Index to Periodical Literature."

Short Story Index—H. W. Wilson, (1953) Includes short story anthologies and magazines published since the early 1950s. Stories filed by author, title, and subject.

Social Sciences Index—New York: Wilson (1974—) Quarterly with annual cumulations. Author and subject index to periodicals in the fields of anthropology, area studies, economics, environmental sciences, political sciences, psychology, public administration, sociology, and related subjects. Indexes about 307 English-language periodicals.

U. S. Government Research and Development Reports—Clearinghouse for Federal Scientific and Technical Information (1946—). Monthly. Abstracting and announcement bulletin covering reports, including progress reports of R&D under government auspices.

Almanacs (yearbooks)

An Almanack—London: J. Whitaker & Sons (1869—). Annual. Major British almanac. Covers British TV, opera, dance, current events, and sciences for the year. Particularly strong in statistics of the British Commonwealth, with brief statistics for other countries.

Hammond Inc. [Hammond World Atlases]. Maplewood, N.J. Hammond, Inc. (1982—). Publishes reputable atlases of the U.S. and foreign countries. U.S. version includes ZIP codes.

Information Please Almanac, Atlas and Yearbook— New York: A & W Publishers (1947—). Annual. More legible and easier to use than the World Almanac, but its coverage is not as complete.

McGraw Hill Yearbook of Science and Technology— McGraw Hill, annual. Reviews the past year's works in science and technology, supplements the McGraw Hill Encyclopedia of Science and Technology.

World Almanac and Book of Facts—New York, Newspaper Enterprise Association (1868—). Annual. Reports major news events of previous year, plus statistical data. Often cited as the best-selling American reference work, as well as the most comprehensive almanac, and most frequently useful.

Atlases

Atlas of the Classical World—Heyden, A.A. and Scullard, Howard Hayes. London: Nelson (1959). Depicts life and cultures of classical world in maps and pictures with textual comment.

Atlas of American History—Jackson, Kenneth T., ed. New York: Scribner (1978). Revision of 1943 edition. Maps include new 20th Century developments including Utopian experiments, women's suffrage, various economic developments, etc.

Goode's World Atlas—Espenshade, Edward B. Jr., ed. Chicago: Rand McNally (1983). Emphasizes physical and political maps and maps showing resources and products. U.S. is given sections, but not by states. Index of more than 30,000 names indicate pronunciation.

Hammond's Ambassador World Atlas—Separate maps of all U.S. states and Canadian provinces. A comprehensive index keys place names to maps so you can quickly locate any town, city, state, river, country, etc. Much geographical data on major world cities is included.

Historical Atlas—Shepherd, William Robert, 9th ed. New York: Barnes & Noble (1964). Excellent one-volume atlas covering the world from about 1945 D.C. to 1964. For many years, it was the standard and most used historical atlas. Each map arranged chronologically. Index of place names, including classical and medieval Latin place names. Cross-referenced to modern form of name.

Rand McNally Cosmopolitan World Atlas —Separate maps of all U.S. states and Canadian provinces. A comprehensive index keys place names to maps so you can quickly locate any town, city, state, river or country. Much geographical data on major world cities is included.

Bibliographies

Bibliographic Index: A Cumulative Bibliography of Bibliographies—New York: H. W. Wilson (1938—). Alphabetical subject arrangement of separately published bibliographies as well as bibliographies published in books and periodicals, many in foreign languages.

A World Bibliography of Bibliographies and of Bibliographical Catalogues, Calendars, Abstracts, Digests, Indexes and The Like—Besterman, Theodore A., Lausanne: Societas Bibliographica, (1965-1966), 5 vol. A cumulative bibliography of bibliographies published in books and manuscripts. International in scope. A massive work. Updated by Toomey's two volume supplement.

World Bibliography of Bibliographies—Toomey, Alice F. (1964-1974) Totowa, N.J.: Rowman & Littlefield (1977), 2 vol. A list of works represented by Library of Congress printed catalog cards. A decennial supplement to Besterman.

Biographies

Author Biographies Master Index—Detroit: Gale Research (1978), supplements, (1979). Consolidated guide to information on authors living and dead as they appear in major biographical dictionaries.

Biography Index: A Cumulative Index to Biographical Material in Books and Magazines—H. W. Wilson, Quarterly (1946—). Key index to biographical material in 1,500 periodicals and books. Lists persons by name and by profession or occupation with reference to all biographical material appearing in current books and periodicals. The most comprehensive index in the field. Arranged alphabetically by the name of the subject of the biography.

Chamber's Biographical Dictionary—Thorne, J.O., and Collocott, T.C., eds. New York: Hippocrene Books (1974). A good dictionary covering the great of all nations, both living and dead.

Current Biography—New York: H.W. Wilson (1940—). Monthly except December, with annual accumulations. Contains lengthy, unbiased biographies written in the manner of a New Yorker profile of almost all Americans and many foreigners who attain a degree of fame.

Cyclopedia of World Authors—Magill, Frank N., ed. Englewood Cliffs, N.J.: Salem press, (1974), 3 vol. Covers authors whose works are included in Masterplots. Each entry gives biographical details, critical evaluation, and a list of the author's published works.

Dictionary of American Biography—New York: Scribner's, (1926—). 17 vol. plus supplements. Noted for its scholarly articles and objectivity. Covers only famous Americans of the past.

Twentieth Century Authors—Kunitz, S.J., Haycraft, H., and Colby, V. New York: H.W. Wilson (1942). First supplement (1955). Biographies and portrait photographs with emphasis on professional men and women whose vocation is writing books of fiction, poetry, history, biography, etc.

Webster's Biographical Dictionary—A Dictionary of Names of Noteworthy Persons with Pronunciations and Concise Biographies. Springfield, MA; Merriam, (1972). A pronouncing biographical dictionary of upwards of 40,000 names, including living persons. Gives brief biographical sketches.

Who's Who in America—Marquis (1899-biennial). Best known and most useful general dictionary of contemporary biography. Entries contain high points in the lives of living Americans who have achieved a degree of importance. Includes birth-date, marriages, names of children, office and home addresses, positions held, etc. People included from all fields, science, education, business, etc.

World Who's Who in Technology Today—J. Dick (1984). 5 vol. Covers electronics and computer science, physics and optics, chemistry and biotechnology, mechanical and civil engineering, energy and earth sciences.

Who's Who in the West—Chicago: Marquis (1949—). Biographical dictionary of noteworthy men and women of the Pacific coastal and Western states.

Books

If the information you're searching for is in a book, a number of potential sources exist for locating the book, in addition to using an electronic or manual card catalog.

Book Review Digest—New York: H. H. Wilson (1905—). Gives digests of book reviews taken from some 75 American and English general-interest magazines. Arranged by title, it carries title and subject indexes.

Book Review Index—Gale Research Co. (1965—). Author index to reviews of books in more than 450 general interest magazines.

Books in Print—New York: R. R. Bowker (1948—). Annual, with supplements. Lists books that are in print from some 3,600 publishers and which can be purchased. Has author, title, and subject listings in separate volumes.

Cumulative Book Index—H. W. Wilson (1898—). Lists by subject and author books in print in the English language of general interest, including the sciences. Arranged by author, title, and subject.

Forthcoming Books—New York: R. R. Bowker (1966—) Bimonthly. Lists books to be published in the succeeding five months by trade publishers. Has author and title listed and a companion bimonthly "Subject Guide to

Forthcoming Books." However, some titles that are announced for publication are never published.

Paperbound Books In Print—New York: R. R. Bowker (1955—) Lists by author, title, and subject in-print paperbacks chiefly from U.S. publishers.

Publishers' Trade List Annual—New York: R. R. Bowker (1873—) Collection of current lists of American and a few Canadian trade publishers, including some university presses and scientific and learned societies. Does not include all publishers.

Reader's Encyclopedia—Benet, William Rose. New York: Crowell (1965). 1 vol. Covers a wide amount of information on books, literary characters and terms, and authors. Also included are references in the fields of art, music, and mythology.

Dictionaries—Abridged

American Heritage Dictionary of the English Language—Boston: Houghton Mifflin. (1982). 1,568p. About 200,000 definitions. Emphasis is placed on offering good usage. Shows proper names and geographical entries. Provides some etymology.

Dictionary Buying Guide—Kister, Kenneth F. New York: R. R. Bowker (1977). Has complete, detailed information on the many excellent dictionaries that are available. Offers information on the best dictionary to use and to purchase for your needs.

Random House College Dictionary—New York: Random House, (1975). Has many illustrations. Strives for modern American English.

Webster's New World Dictionary of the American Language—New York: Simon and Schuster, (1980). 150,000 entries includes proper names, place-names, abbreviations, foreign phrases all included in one alphabet. Has pronunciation and etymology. Includes idiomatic and slang terms.

Webster's Ninth New Collegiate Dictionary—Springfield, Mass.: Merriam, (1983). Nearly 160,000 entries and 200,000 definitions. Definitions in chronological order.

Dictionaries—Unabridged

Oxford English Dictionary (OED)—Clarendon Press. A classic! A WARNING—you can easily get captivated when using this fascinating dictionary. It is the most authoritative dictionary of the English language and gives the etymology or history of the words.

The Compact Edition of the Oxford English Dictionary—James Murray et. al., ed., (New York: Oxford University press, 1971). Comes in two volumes but contains the same information as the big one. Print size is so small that a magnifying glass is provided with the two volumes. An excellent buy!

Random House Dictionary of the English Language—New York: Random House, (1966) 2,059p. More than 260,000 entries, encyclopedic scope of entries. Includes several foreign word lists and an atlas section.

Webster's New International Dictionary of the English Language—Springfield, Mass.: Merriam, (1961). 319p. Oldest and most famous American dictionary, well rounded, reliable. Definitions given in historical sequence. 600,000 entries.

Webster's Third New International Dictionary of the English Language. Springfield, MA: Merriam, (1961). 2,600 pages. Can be used for years, even decades.

Drama

The Encyclopedia of World Theater—Edited with an introduction by Martin Esslin. New York: Scribner's, (1977). With 420 illustrations and an index of play titles.

Play Index—(1949-82). Wilson. Locates monologues, pantomimes, and one-act and full-length plays published in anthologies, and as single volumes. Plays are listed by author, title, and subject.

The Reader's Encyclopedia of World Drama—Gassner, John and Quinn, Edward. New York: Crowell, (1969). 1030p. One-volume book with emphasis on drama as literature. Has information on plays and playwrights from all countries and an appendix containing basic documents in dramatic theory.

Encyclopedias—General interest

"Encyclopedia" is from the Greek and means "circle of knowledge." It is an ancient form of reference book, the oldest was the 37-volume "Natural History" of Pliny the Elder (circa 23-79 A.D.).

If you know little or nothing about your topic, this is often a good place to start. Occasionally these have excellent summaries on what you're looking for and, more importantly, good references to other documents having greater depth. Usually they're well cross-referenced. Encyclopedias are usually more up-to-date than books since they're revised more often.

Academic American—Princeton: Arete Pub. Co., 21 vol. Falls somewhere between the *World Book* and the *Britannica* in scope and depth of treatment. The full text of the encyclopedia is available on-line through a number of commercial vendors. Intended for students in junior high, high school, college, and inquisitive adults.

Americana—New York: Encyclopedia Americana, 30 vol. Full and scholarly. Strong on American topics, especially strong in science and technology. Good, comprehensive encyclopedia for general use.

Britannica—Chicago: Encyclopedia Britannica, (1983). 30 vol. First published as a 3-volume set in 1771. Full and scholarly. Good coverage of both British and American topics. The most famous encyclopedia in English.

Colliers Encyclopedia—New York: Macmillan. 24 vol. Emphasis on simple explanations. Strong in contemporary science. Third in size to Americana and Britannica, but is the most current, best indexed, and easiest to read of the three. Style is popular, clear and concise.

Encyclopedia Buying Guide: A Consumer Guide to General Encyclopedias in Print—Kister, Kenneth, New York: R. R. Bowker, (1981). Covers all aspects of encyclopedias—arrangement, scope, history, bibliography, etc. Refers readers to other critical opinions and reviews.

Funk and Wagnalls New Encyclopedia—Funk and Wagnalls. 27 vol. (1984). Serves general family needs. Provides brief background on a wide variety of topics and is written in a clear, popular style. Useful, inexpensive choice.

Lincoln Library of Essential Information—Buffalo, NY: Frontier Press (1985). 2 vol. Arranged in 12 broad topical sections called departments. Each department, such as biography and mathematics, has a series of essays arranged in A to Z order.

The New Columbia Encyclopedia—New York: Columbia University Press, (1975). 1 vol. Capsule size for quick reference. Contains some 50,000 articles, maps, and line drawings, more separate entries than most English language encyclopedias.

World Book—Chicago: Field Enterprises Corp., 22 vol. Ranges from young people to general adult in content, keyed to school curricula.

Government publications

Government Reference Books. (1968-69—). Published every two years by Libraries Unlimited. Covers pamphlets, books, bibliographies, directories, and other government publications in all subjects. Arranged by broad subject category with separate subject and title indexes.

Guide to Popular U. S. Government Publications— Libraries Unlimited, (1986). 432p. References 2,900 titles of government documents, most of which have been published since 1978, with a brief description of each document's contents.

Monthly Catalog of U. S. Government Publications— U.S. Govt. Printing Office (1895—). Comprehensive index. Lists all publications of all government departments, bureaucracies, and agencies. Published monthly, with annual cumulative index. Gives author, title, publication data, price, and availability. Does not include classified documents.

Subject Guide to U.S. Government Reference Sources—American Library Association (1985). Subject index, plus a directory. Annotated bibliography of key government documents on general topics, more than 1,300 entries, includes science and technology.

U.S. Government Reports Announcement and Index—U.S. Dept. of Commerce, National Technical Information Service (NTIS) (1971—). Semimonthly, with annual accumulations. Indexes and abstracts unclassified reports of U.S. Government contractors in public and private sector. Indexed by individual and corporate author, subject, report number, and accession number.

History

Dictionary of American History. 8 vol. Adams, James T. New York: Charles Scribners' Sons, (1976). Concise articles on a wide variety of subject in American life and history. Most entries have brief bibliography of more extensive works on the subject.

Chronology of World History: A Calendar of Principal Events from 3000 BC to AD. Dist. by Rowman & Littlefield (1978). London, Collings. 2 ed.

Encyclopedia of World History—Langer, William Leonard, 5th ed. Boston: Houghton Mifflin (1972) 2 vol. Arranged chronologically—by ages—and within each time period it covers geographical areas. Indexed with many maps.

The Historian's Handbook: A Descriptive Guide to Reference Works—Poulton, Helen. Norman, OK: University of Oklahoma Press (1972). Bibliographic guide to major reference sources for the student and beginning researcher. Includes library catalogs, statistical guides, almanacs, newspaper indexes, quotation dictionaries, etc.

Language—Style and usage

The Elements of Style. Strunk, Wm. Revised by E.B. White. New York: Macmillan (1979). An excellent, compact reference on style. If you only own one book on style, this should be the one.

A Manual of Style—Chicago: University of Chicago Press (1982). Style manual for authors, editors, and copywriters. Standard reference work.

Libraries—How to locate one

American Library Directory—R. R. Bowker Co. (1923—) Annual, with supplement. Lists more than 30,000 U.S. and Canadian libraries of all kinds, including public, academic, company, museum, newspaper, special subject, private historical society, hospital, church, military, government, association, etc. Arranged alphabetically by state but has no subject index.

Directory of Historical Societies and Agencies in the United States and Canada—American Association for State and Local History. Issued every three years. Names historical and genealogical societies in the U.S. and Canada.

Research Centers Directory—Detroit: Gale Research Co. (1960—). Published every three to four years with supplements. Guide to university-related and other non-profit research organizations established on a permanent basis and carrying on continuing research programs.

Subject Collections—by Ash, Lee, R. R. Bowker Co. (1978). Published about every five to seven years. Identifies the subject collections of university, college, public, museum, historical society and special libraries and museums in the U.S. and Canada.

Writer's Resource Guide edited by Bernadine Clark. Writer's Digest Books. Excellent resource. Updated about every three years. Lists foundations, associations, government agencies, companies, museums, historical societies, and special collections with information on the services provided, how to contact them, and more. Arranged in subject categories and indexed by subject and organization name.

Newspapers

National Newspaper Index—(1979—). Information Access Corp. Monthly. Microfilm index of five of the country's major newspapers for the past three years: The New York Times, The Christian Science Monitor, The Wall Street Journal, the Los Angeles Times, and the Washington Post. Indexing is cover-to-cover except for weather charts, horoscopes, crossword puzzles, and stock market tables.

The New York Times Index—New York: The New York Times (1913—). Indexes all articles published in The New York Times, preserved on microfilm and carefully indexed by subject alphabetically. Each entry provides a reference to date, page number, and column number. Available for almost every year back to 1851, covering both daily and Sunday issues. Semi-monthly with annual accumulations.

The Official Index of the Times—London: The Times Publishing Co. (1906—) Alphabetically arranged by subjects, organizations, and people and under each heading, according to the dates of occurrences, the index is based on the final daily editions of the London Times. Recommended for research on British news.

People

Authors of articles. Why not contact the author of one or more of the reports or books in your field of interest that you found particularly informative? He or she will usually cooperate and bring you up-to-date on what has been happening since the article was published.

Encyclopedia of Associations—Gale Research Company (1956—). 5 vol. Excellent reference. Lists some 18,000 national and international organizations of virtually every field imaginable. An excellent source for locating experts in various associations. Includes scientific, engineering, and technical associations. Has key word, geographical, and executive index, research activities, and funding programs.

Magazine editors. They're an excellent source, not only for information about what's going on in a certain field, but they can also direct you to experts in your specialty.

People at other companies. Often even your competitors will consult with you on a problem, particularly if it's on a person-to-person basis, rather than on a company-to-company.

Your librarian. They're always willing to help and can locate even the most obscure facts, or anything you need, in books you never even dreamed existed.

Your fellow employees. Check around your company, you may find an expert or two.

Periodicals

When you need to search specific periodicals in your field of interest, the books listed below will help you locate the names and addresses of such periodicals.

Gale Directory of Publications—(Formerly Ayer Directory of Publications) Gale Research, Inc. (1989). Index of 25,000 newspapers and magazines published in the U. S. and Canada, and a few foreign countries.

Reader's Guide to Periodical Literature. New York: H.W. Wilson, (1900—). A modern index of the best type. Indexes U.S. periodicals of a broad, general, and popular character. About 174 periodicals are indexed.

Standard Periodical Directory—Oxbridge (1964/65—). The largest authoritative guide to U.S. and Canadian publications, information on more than 65,000 publications. Alphabetical arrangement, with index of titles and subjects.

Ulrich's International Periodical Directory—R. R. Bowker (1932—). 2 vol. Lists more than 70,000 currently published periodicals from more than 120 countries. Grouped by subject, with title and subject indexes. The most comprehensive of scientific (especially scholarly) publications from around the world. Also cites the indexing or abstracting services for each periodical. A very valuable reference.

Publishers

Editor and Publisher Market Guide—New York: Editor and Publisher (1924—). Annual. Lists American cities, where daily newspapers are published, under geographical arrangement, giving type of community, location, population, retail and wholesale outlets, colleges and universities, number of telephones and car registrations, per-capita income, newspapers and other information.

International Directory of Little Magazines and Small Presses—Paradise, Calif.: Dustbooks (1973—) Annual. Lists little magazines and small presses and includes comments by the editors regarding policy and types of material and lists of recent contributors.

Literary Market Place—New York: Bowker. (1940—) Annual. Lists book publishers and magazines with addresses, editors' names and brief information on the types of material they publish. Also lists book clubs, agents, awards, etc. An excellent reference.

Writer's Market—Cincinnati, Ohio: Writer's Digest (1930—) Annual. Describes markets for writers such as book publishers, magazine, consumer publications, script-writing, trade, technical, and professional markets.

Statistics

American Statistics Index—Washington: Congressional Information Service. (1973—). Comprehensive guide and index to publications of U.S. Government agencies.

Index to International Statistics—(1983—). Indexes statistics that appear in the publications of more than 30 UN agencies and commissions.

Statistical Abstracts of the United States—U.S. Department of Commerce, Bureau of Census, Washington, D.C.: Government Printing Office (1879—). Annual. Most tables go back for about 20 years. Provides statistics on virtually every topic of public interest including industrial, social, political, economic, and cultural activities.

Statistical Reference Index—(1980—). Locates statistics issued by commercial publishers, associations, businesses, university research centers, and some state agencies.

Statistics Sources—Wasserman, Paul and O'Brien, Jacqueline, eds. 9th ed. Detroit: Gale (1984) 2 vol. Subject guide to data on social, industrial, business, financial, and other topics for the U.S. and internationally.

Addresses of On-line Vendors

Applelink—Quantum Computer Services, Inc.
8619 Westwood Center Dr.
Vienna, VA 2180
703-448-8700

BRS Information Technologies
8000 Westpark Drive
McLean, VA 22102
800-955-0906/703-442-0900

Compuserve Information Services
5000 Arlington Centre Blvd.
P.O. Box 20212
Columbus, OH 43220
614-457-8600/800-848-8199

Delphi
3 Blackstone Street
Cambridge, MA 02139
800-544-4005/617 491-3342

Dialog Information Services, Inc.
3460 Hillview Avenue
Palo Alto, CA 94304
415-858-3785
800-3-DIALOG

Dow Jones
P.O. Box 300
Princeton, NJ 08543-0300
609-452-1511/800-522-3567

**GEnie
General Electric Information Services**
401 N. Washington Street
Rockville, MD 20850
301-340-4000/800-638-9636

Knowledge Index
415-858-3785
800-334-2564

Mead Data Central
9393 Springboro Pike
P.O. Box 933
Dayton, OH 45401
513-865-6800
800-227-4908

NEWSNET
945 Haverford Road
Bryn Mawr, PA 19010
215-527-8030
800-345-1301

Orbit Search Service
8000 Westpark Drive
McLean, VA 22102
703-442-0900
800-456-7248

Prodigy
445 Hamilton Avenue
White Plains, NY 10601
914-993-8000
800-822-6922

VU/TEXT
Information Services, Inc.
325 Chestnut Street
Suite 1300
Philadelphia, PA 19106
215-574-4400
800-323-2940

Appendix C

Bibliography

Adams, James L. *The Care & Feeding of Ideas*. Addison-Wesley, Reading, Mass., 1986

Blicq, R.S. *Technically—Write!* Prentice Hall, Englewood Cliffs, N.J., 1972

Campbell, Walter S. (Stanley Vestal) *Writing Non-Fiction*. The Writer, Boston, 1961.

Emerson, Connie. *Write On: Target*, Writer's Digest, Cincinnati, Ohio, 1981

Ferrarini, Elizabeth. *Infomania*. Houghton Mifflin, Boston, 1985

Glossbrenner, Alfred. *How to Look it up Online*. St. Martins Press, New York, 1987

Glossbrenner, Alfred. *Personal Computer Communications*. St. Martins Press, New York, 1985

Glover, John A. *Becoming a More Creative Person*. Prentice-Hall, Englewood Cliffs, N.J. 1980

Helliwell, John. *Inside Information*, New American Library, New York, 1986

Li, Tze-chung. *An Introduction to Online Searching*. Greenwood Press, Westport, Conn., 1985

Swain, Dwight V. *Techniques of the Selling Writer*. University of Oklahoma Press, Norman, Okla, 1965.

Index

The Write Stuff

American Library Directory, 102
American Men and Women of Science, 107
American Reference Books Annual, 106
Analogy, 46
Anecdotes, 189-190
Aristotle, 117, 155
    laws of association, 141
Association, 141

Bacon, Francis, 98
Bibliographic Index, 106
Body, 119-120
    chapter, 127-128
    conflict, 123
    dilemma, 124
    magic three, 32
    nonfiction, 122
Boileau, Nicolas, 166
Bookstores, research, 106
Bottom-up writing, 12f, 155-168
    brainstorming, 157
    cull, 158
    examples of, 169-179
    judge, 157-158
    ordinate, 159

    precedent sort, 160
    revising, 166-168
    subroutine, 33
Brainstorming, 31, 71-89, 157
    asking questions, 85-88
    defined, 82
    example of, 85-87
    personal computer, 84
    process of, 83
    top-down design, 138
Bubble sort, computer sorting, 29, 50

Card catalog, 103-104
Carlyle, Thomas, 91, 97
Categorization, organizing writing, 37
Cause-to-effect order, 39
    example of, 42
Chapter, fiction structure, 128
Chronological order, 39
Churchill, Sir Winston, 183
Climactic order, 39, 45
Coleridge, Samuel T., 49, 118
Comparison-by-pairs, precedent sort, 50
Comparison-contrast order, 39

Computer,
  bubble sort, 29
  structured programming, 28
  top-down programming, 28
Computer programming
  procedures, 18
  relationship to writing, 134
Computer subroutine, 132
Conclusion, 119-120
  chapter, 128
  decision, 124
  disaster, 123
  magic three, 32
  nonfiction, 122
Conflict, body, 123
Creativity, 71-89
Creativity, Research on, 72
  alpha waves, 72
  characteristics of, 74
  cultivating, 72
  dormancy, 75
  planning, 74
  process, 32
  writing, 16

Database, 113
  advantages of, 114-115
Davis, Richard Harding, 109
Dawson, G. 102
Decision, conclusion, 124
Deductive order, 44-45
Department of Energy,
  information source, 107
Dilemma, body, 124
*Directory of Historical Societies
  and Agencies in the United
  States and Canada*, 103
*Directory of Special Libraries and
  Information Centers*, 103
Disaster, conclusion, 123
Discontent, characteristic of
  creativity, 79

Edison, Thomas, 79-80, 81
Effect-to-cause order,
  example of, 42
Electronic card catalogs, 104-105

Electronic libraries, 32
*Encyclopedia of Associations,
  The*, 107
Evinrude, Ole, 79

Faculty Directory, 107
Faraday, Michael, 80
Fiction module, 17
  defined, 18
Fog index, 192-194
France, Anatole, 187
Franklin, Benjamin, 182

General references, research, 105
General-to-specific order, 44-45
Goal, introduction, 123
Goethe, 76
Government Reference Books,
  106
Grammar, 185
Grummond, Chester, 78
Guide to Reference Books, 106

Hawthorne, Nathaniel, 181
How-to order, 39, 45

Increasing detail order, 44
Increasing-to-decreasing order, 39
Increasing/decreasing importance
  order, 43-44
Index cards, taking notes, 110
Inductive order, 44
Information, mail, 108
Information sources, 98-108
Introduction, 119-120
  chapter, 127
  goal, 123
  magic three, 32
  reaction, 124

Johnson, Samuel, 57, 100, 129
Joubert, Joseph, 80

Kipling, Rudyard, 84
Known-to-unknown order, 39, 46

L'Enfant, Pierre Charles, 77

Library,
    effective use of, 32
    electronic, 32
Library of Congress,
    research, 107
Logical order, 39
    examples of, 42-45
Longinus, 38

Magic Three, 13, 32, 117-130
    book, 128-129
    chapter, 127-128
    modules, 121
    paragraphs, 119-121
    sentences, 118-119
Major division order, 39, 41
Modular writing, 11ff, 17
    technique, 17
    unlimited use, 24
    writer's block, 24
Module, 23, 121
    fiction, 17, 123
    nonfiction, 17
    scene, 123
    sequel, 124
Mozart, 82

National Referral Center,
    research, 107
Natural order, 39, 40
Niebuhr, Reinhold, 74
Nonfiction module, 17
    defined, 18
Numerical/alphabetical order, 39
    example of, 40-41

Online databases, 13
    information source, 98
Online systems, 32
    research, 113
Operational order, 45
Order,
    analogy, 46
    cause-to-effect, 42
    climactic, 45
    comparison/contrast, 43
    deductive, 44-45

effect-to-cause, 42
general-to-specific, 44-45
how-to-do-it, 45
increasing detail, 44
inductive, 44
known-to-unknown, 46
logical, 42-45
major division, 41
natural, 40
numerical/alphabetical, 40-41
operational, 45
psychological, 45
reversible, 39
spatial, 40-41
specific-to-general, 44
suspense, 45
which to use, 46-47
Ordering,
    fiction example, 62-66
    nonfiction example, 57-62
    organizing writing, 37
    pattern, natural, 39
Ordering patterns, 38, 39-46
Ordering sequences, 139
    chapter to chapter, 139
    module to module, 139
    submodule to submodule, 139
Ordinate, bottom-up writing, 159
Organization,
    benefits of, 27
    clarity, 19
    importance of, 26
    new technique, 28
    steps required, 37
    writing, 19
Organizing and outlining,
    complaints about, 20
Originality, characteristic of
    creativity, 77
Orwell, George, 81, 182
Outline, 20, 36, 156
    benefits of, 22f
    advantages of, 24, 25
    types of, 37
Outlining,
    enhances creativity, 23
    importance of, 22

Paragraphs,
  fiction, 121
  nonfiction, 119-121
Parallelism, sentence structure,
  118-119
Paraphrasing, research, 109
Pasteur, Louis, 74, 78
Pauling, Linus, 71
Personal computer, 16, 32
  brainstorming on, 84
  writer's tool, 91-96
Personal library, information
  source, 98
Planning, importance of, 36
Pope, Alexander, 19
Precedent Sort, 11ff, 17, 30,
  49-56, 110
  advantages of, 29
  bottom-up writing, 160
  bubble sort, 50
  caution, 68
  comparison-by-pairs, 50
  example, 30, 50-55
  fiction example, 62-66
  guidelines for use, 67
  nonfiction example, 57-62
  principle of fewness, 49
  subjective process, 68
Princeton University, creativity
  research, 72
Principle of fewness, 49
Pro/con order, 39, 45
Programming, computer, 18
Psychological order, 39, 45
Punctuation, 188
Pythagoras, 117

Reaction, sequel, 124
Readability, 192
Reference sources, books on,
  105-106
Relationships, ordering
  sequences, 139
Research, 97-115
  bookstores, 106
  card catalog, 103-104
  electronic, 104-105

general references, 105
getting started, 102
ideas, 32
locating experts, 106-107
online systems, 113
paraphrasing, 109
plagiarism, 109
questions to ask, 98-100
reviewing books, 112
taking notes, 109-112
Retention curve, 190-191
Reversible order, 39
Reviewing books, research, 112
Roman numerals, outlining, 20

Scene,
  fiction module, 18
  module, 123
Schopenhauer, Arthur, 131
Sentence outline, 37, 38
Sequel,
  fiction module, 18
  module, 124
Sequence, writing, 23
Spatial order, 39, 40-41
Specific-to-general order, 39, 44
Spelling, 186
Stevenson, Robert L., 35, 169
Strunk, William, Jr., 181
Subject Guide to Books in Print,
  107
Subroutine, writing, 132
  fiction, figure, 145
Summary of book, 30-33
Suspense order, 45

Tagore, Rabindranath, 19
Taking notes,
  index cards, 110
  research, 109-112
Tesla, Nikola, 72-73
Top-down design, 12f, 131-144
  article, 150-153
  brainstorming, 138
  examples, 145-153
  judge/cull, 142
  order, 133

ordering sequences, 139
organize/order, 142
planning subroutine, 33
preliminary research, 137
principles, 18
short story, 146-150
subcomponent topics, 140
title/theme/purpose, 135
universal subroutine, 134
update outline, 143
Top-down programming,
    computer, 28
Topic outline, 37-38
Transitions, 124-127, 187-188
    bottom-up writing, 166
    table, 125

U.S. Government Manual, 107
Upjohn, W. John, 75

Vocabulary, understanding, 184
Voltaire, 32

Who's Who in America, 107
Word order, 184
Word processor, 91
    advantages of, 91-93
    basic capabilities, 93-96
    block move, 94
    boldface, 94
    cancel/pause print, 95
    centering, 94
    contents/index generation, 95
    copy, 94
    delete, 94
    diskette storage, 95
    double-column printing, 95
    full justify, 94
    graphics, 94
    help menu, 93

insert mode, 93
line length, 94
macros, 95
oops! command, 94
positive writing attitude, 92
print, 94
print spooling, 95
search, 94
search and replace, 94
speller, 95
tab set, 94
thesaurus, 95
underline, 94
word count, 95
Word-processing programs,
    16-17, 32
Words,
    emotion, 183
    understanding, 182
    use of big, 189
*World Bibliography of
    Bibliographies, A.,* 105
Writer's block, 12, 24
Writers' Resource Guide, 103
Writing,
    basic steps, 25
    bottom-up, 160-165
    clarity, 19
    creative aspects of, 16
    definition of good, 181-182
    difficulties of, 29-30
    random sequence, 23
    sequence of, 23
    subroutine, 132
    techniques, 181-196
    techniques, importance of
    length, 187

Yellow pages, information
    source, 108

LAWRENCE BRANCH